GUINNESS
A FAMILY SUCCESSION

GUINNESS
A FAMILY SUCCESSION

*The True Story of the Struggle
to Create the World's
Largest Brewery*

ARTHUR
EDWARD
GUINNESS

WITH

ANTONIA HART

SCALA

This edition © B.T. Batsford Ltd., 2025
Text © Arthur Edward Guinness 2025

First published in 2025 by
Scala Arts & Heritage Publishers Ltd
43 Great Ormond Street
London WC1N 3HZ, UK
www.scalapublishers.com
An imprint of B. T. Batsford Holdings Ltd.

ISBN (hardback): 978-1-78551-609-2
ISBN (trade paperback): 978-1-78551-633-7

Typesetting and plate section by seagulls.net
Cover design by Eoghan O'Brien
Printed and bound by CPI (UK) Ltd, Croydon CR0 4YY

Scala is represented in UK and Europe by
Abrams & Chronicle Books,
1 West Smithfield, London, EC1A 9JU
and 57 rue Gaston Tessier, 75166 Paris, France.

10 9 8 7 6 5 4 3 2

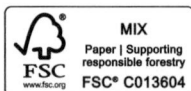

FSC
www.fsc.org
MIX
Paper | Supporting
responsible forestry
FSC® C013604

Frontispiece: Benjamin Lee Guinness, seated right, with his wife
Elizabeth and their children: Arthur and Annie are standing,
Lee is seated left, and Edward Cecil sits at his father's feet.

CONTENTS

Elizabeth Read = Richard Guinness = Elizabeth Clare
of Celbridge
(c.1690–1766)

Arthur Guinness = Olivia Whitmore   Frances   Elizabeth   Benjamin   Richard
(1725–1803)

Frederick = Elizabeth   Rev. Hosea = Jane   **Arthur Guinness (II)** = (1) Anne Lee
Darley   (1765–1841) Hart   (1768–1855)   = (2) Maria Barker

Rev. William = Susan Jane   Arthur Lee   **Sir Benjamin Lee Guinness** = Elizabeth
Smythe Lee   Guinness   (1797–1863)   (1798–1868)
Grattan

Annie = Rev. William Conyngham,   Sir Arthur Edward, = Lady Olivia
        4th Baron Plunkett,   Baron Ardilaun   Hedges-White
        Archbishop of Dublin   (1840–1915)

Sir Rupert Edward = Lady Gwendolen
Cecil Lee Guinness, Onslow CBE
2nd Earl of Iveagh
(1874–1967)

Richard   Lady Honor = Henry (Chips)   Hon. Arthur = Lady Elizabeth
           Dorothy   Channon MP   Onslow Edward, Hare
                                         Viscount Elveden
                                         (1912–1945)

Sir Arthur Francis = Miranda Smiley   Lady Eliza
Benjamin Guinness,   (b.1939)
3rd Earl of Iveagh
(1937–1992)

Lady Emma Lavinia   Lady Louisa Jane
(b.1963)   (b.1967)

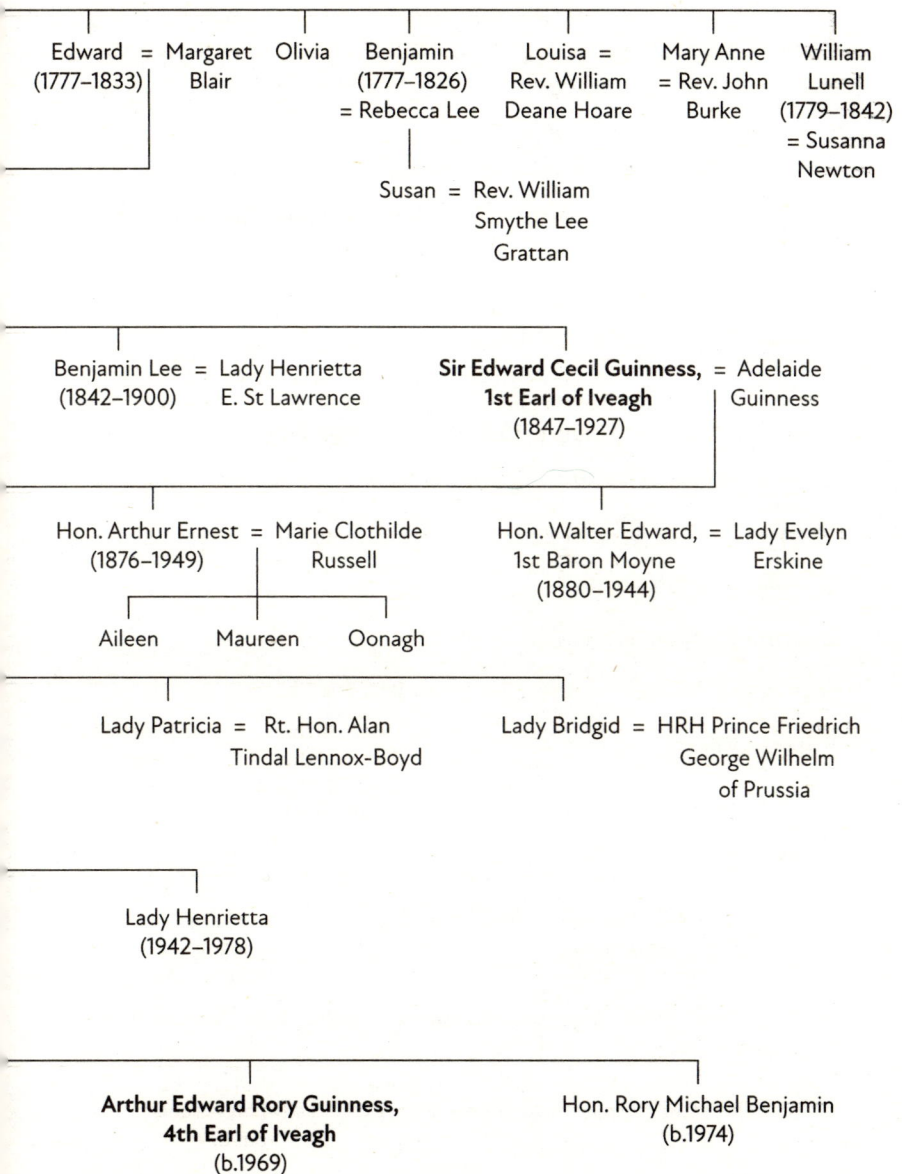

FAMILY TREE

Edward = Margaret   Olivia   Benjamin   Louisa =   Mary Anne   William
(1777–1833) Blair   (1777–1826)   Rev. William   = Rev. John   Lunell
                                  = Rebecca Lee   Deane Hoare   Burke   (1779–1842)
                                                                                = Susanna
                                                                                  Newton

Susan = Rev. William
        Smythe Lee
        Grattan

Benjamin Lee = Lady Henrietta   **Sir Edward Cecil Guinness,** = Adelaide
(1842–1900)   E. St Lawrence   **1st Earl of Iveagh**   Guinness
                                       (1847–1927)

Hon. Arthur Ernest = Marie Clothilde   Hon. Walter Edward, = Lady Evelyn
(1876–1949)   Russell   1st Baron Moyne   Erskine
                                              (1880–1944)

Aileen   Maureen   Oonagh

Lady Patricia = Rt. Hon. Alan   Lady Bridgid = HRH Prince Friedrich
                Tindal Lennox-Boyd   George Wilhelm
                                                      of Prussia

Lady Henrietta
(1942–1978)

Arthur Edward Rory Guinness,   Hon. Rory Michael Benjamin
4th Earl of Iveagh   (b.1974)
(b.1969)

ILLUSTRATION CREDITS

Plate numbers ('P') refer to the page of the plate section on which that image appears.

All images are from Guinness family archives except for the following, which are reproduced by kind permission:

AA Images/Alamy: P8 (bottom)

Creative Commons via National Gallery of Ireland: P3 (bottom)

Guinness Archive, Diageo Ireland: 18, 50, 104, 138, P1 (top right, bottom), P2 (bottom), P3 (top), P4 (top left, top right), P5 (both), P6 (top), P7 (top), P9 (top), P14 (top)

Antonia Hart: 4, P2 (top left), P10 (top)

History Collection/Alamy: P6 (bottom)

Angelo Hornak/Alamy: P16 (top left)

© National Portrait Gallery, London: P16 (top left)

Robert O'Byrne: P2 (top right)

The Picture Art Collection/Alamy: P11 (top right)

Public domain via Getty Museum: 68, 86

Public domain via Library of Congress: P9 (bottom)

Public domain: P8 (top)

© Royal Collection Enterprises Limited 2025 | Royal Collection Trust: P12

Wikimedia Commons (Wellcome Collection): P15 (top)

NOTE ON NAMES

In order to keep things simple, and in an effort not to interrupt the narrative too much, I have generally used my family's Christian names throughout. As if the complications of changing titles weren't enough, generations of my family have featured a disproportionate number of Arthurs, Benjamins and Edwards. I have adopted the following simplified usage for the purposes of this book:

Arthur Guinness (1725–1803), usually Arthur and sometimes for clarity Arthur I.

Arthur Guinness (1768–1855), usually Arthur and sometimes for clarity Arthur II.

Benjamin Lee Guinness (1798–1868), later Sir Benjamin Lee Guinness, first Baronet, usually Benjamin Lee.

Arthur Edward Guinness (1840–1915), later Sir Arthur Guinness, second Baronet, later Baron Ardilaun, usually Arthur, sometimes, as in correspondence, Lord Ardilaun.

Edward Cecil Guinness (1847–1927), later Sir Edward Guinness, later Baron Iveagh of Iveagh, later Viscount Iveagh, later the Earl of Iveagh, usually Ned, sometimes Edward or Edward Cecil, or, as in correspondence, Lord Iveagh.

Portrait of the author as a young man at Farmleigh,
reading Martelli's *Man of His Time*.

PROLOGUE

I was born and raised in Farmleigh House, my great-great-grandparents' country house outside Dublin, which today serves as the Official Irish State Guesthouse. As a child, I lived with the stories and the fabric of life gathered from an age past alongside those of the present.

As a family we adapted this beautiful and comfortable home to our own pattern of use. We enjoyed fireside conversations in the Boudoir, and opening presents at Christmas in the Blue Drawing Room. The waft of my father's cigar down the corridor, the delights of playing in the farmyard, tasting apples in the orchard, or relishing fruits and vegetables grown in the Walled Garden.

Farmleigh was my life and that of my siblings, built in another age and tailored to the present. The character of my great-great-grandparents, Edward and Adelaide, the 1st Earl and Countess of Iveagh, was etched into this glorious homestead. I was always fascinated to understand the reasons: why were we there? Why did we live as we did, surrounded by a disparate array of wonderful persons who made Farmleigh work so well? The quiet pride of those who served my family on a shared mission, and with one consistent value – kindness. Each corner of Farmleigh held stories. Some were secret, like folklore; some real; whilst others were imagined or exaggerated or made up.

I reached an age when I was introduced to the family historical bible, George Martelli's book *Man of His Time*, about my great-great-grandfather Edward, which had been privately published in 1957. I cherished it, reading of the lives and characters of those forebears it highlighted, and it helped me to

understand what happened, and why I lived as I did. Rupert
Guinness, my great-grandfather, writes in its prologue:

> I commissioned this book because I thought that my
> father's descendants should have a record of his life, what
> he did and the times he lived in so that those who inherit
> the fortune he built may understand its foundations.

Today we are an ever more numerous family, as the branches
have extended and the generations have grown onwards. I do
not know as many of my cousins Guinness as I might, a position
likely to extend as time passes, and it is time the Guinness story is
told to a wider audience from within.

We Guinnesses have sometimes occupied a rather ambigu-
ous position, not central to the establishment, but on the fringes.
At times this lent itself to loneliness and misunderstanding. But
we have always supported inclusivity and believed in dignity,
fairness and rights for all people equally. We are all stakeholders
in one society. We have always tried to plough our own furrow,
with perception and tenacity. We have done things in our own
distinctive way.

This book attempts to tell the true story and real lives
of the first four Guinness generations for whom beer was the
central focus. Good lives lived, not unblemished by incidents
and accidents, but nonetheless characterised by the Goodness
in Guinness, which luckily for us persisted, despite many challenges. It starts with the origins of the first Arthur Guinness, who
founded the brewery in Dublin in 1759, and finishes with the
death of my great-great-grandfather in 1927. It does not bring
the story all the way up to the present, which would be another
story again. Rather, it honours the toils of my forebears in epic
and convulsive times for Ireland and Britain, and the many others
who have laboured since to ensure that the foundations built by
past generations endure. Legacy is about what we do with it,

how we nurture the best of it and discard those parts that have become moribund.

I hope all enjoy reading this book as much as I have enjoyed and felt gratified by its creation, and that it helps to explain how things became what they are today.

Arthur Edward Guinness
Elveden, Suffolk, June 2025

Plaque marking the site of Arthur Guinness's first brewery in Leixlip.

ONE

ARTHUR'S WAY

If you climb up from the townland of Ardclough, near Straffan in county Kildare, you reach the hilltop spot of Oughterard. The road here used to be the main highway from Dublin to Limerick, and on to Cork. The turnpike built in the early eighteenth century drew that traffic away for good. Now it is all tranquillity, but Oughterard is still remarkable for its round tower, and the walled churchyard around the ruins of a medieval church, which has its own adjoining tower. It bulges, but is supported by concrete buttresses. From the top of the church tower you get a panoramic view of the rich Kildare countryside.

In May 2025, when I last visited, turning this book over in my mind, the view was every kind of green. It had rained so much that spring that the barley was late, later at least than it was at home in Suffolk. But Oughterard has the character of home for me, too. My roots are in this small churchyard with this enormous view. Here, among the graves of the other local people, my great-great-great-great-great-grandfather Arthur Guinness is buried, along with his parents, his wife Elizabeth and 11 of their young children.

As with so many family stories, it is challenging to decide precisely where to begin the Guinness story. You could explore numerous branches of numerous family trees, tracing connection and significance from every fork. This fork in this story has its own trail now. Arthur's Way is a 16-kilometre waymarked walking and cycling route through north-east Kildare, from Leixlip to Celbridge, with a gorgeous stretch along the towpath of the Grand Canal which brings you to Ardclough before that

final leg up the hill to Oughterard. For a man whose memory
is so entwined with the history of Dublin to be buried here at
Oughterard, about 15 miles away, suggests a deep attachment to
a homeplace, entirely separate from his life in the capital.

I wonder whether Arthur perhaps felt some uncertainty
about staying in Dublin, about whether the brewery he founded
there would last; even, after all those infant deaths, whether his
family would survive city life. He does seem to have thought of
Oughterard as home, and intended to return there one day. And,
as it seems that Arthur's connection with beer may have originated not with the Guinnesses but with his mother's family, the
Reads of Oughterard, it seems fitting to pick this tiny 'high place'
(as Uachtar Ard translates), to be the geographical and chrono-
logical starting point for this story of family succession.

Arthur Guinness's maternal grandparents were a farming
couple, and in 1690 his grandfather William Read obtained a
licence to sell ale. My cousin, Patrick Guinness, in his meticulously researched *Arthur's Round*, describes this licence as the
first written proof of any link to beer in the family. William was
on to a good thing. A hundred years earlier, the sixteenth-century
Irish diet had revolved around beer and bread, both satisfying,
and full of essential calories and nutrition. Not only that, but beer
was often safer to drink than water.

The quantities of beer drunk during the working day seem
astonishing four hundred years later. Food historian Susan Flavin,
after immersing herself in household accounts, soldiers' ration
books and other provisioning sources, found that the household
staff of Dublin Castle managed to put away 264,000 pints of beer
in 1590, which averaged eight pints a day per head. Quarrying
stone in Clontarf for Christ Church Cathedral in 1565, the hot
and dusty stonemasons were allowed 14 pints of ale a day to
quench their thirst. It kept their strength up, too, with between
five and seven thousand calories in those 14 pints. Nor was it
some weak and watery beer, because its strength was between

7 and 10 per cent. It seems barely credible that the masons managed to complete a full day's labour on this kind of intake.

The year 1690, when William Read got his licence, is indelibly marked on the Irish psyche as the year of the Battle of the Boyne, when another William, the Protestant King William III, the Dutch Prince of Orange, defeated his father-in-law, the exiled Catholic King James II, who immediately fled to France. This momentous battle happened about 45 miles from Oughterard, in the neighbouring county Meath. A year later the Williamite war ended when the Jacobites surrendered, and many left for France and Spain in what became known as the Flight of the Wild Geese.

Those who stayed at home were promised religious freedom and security in their property, but of course nothing of the kind transpired, and instead there began many years of harsh restrictions on Catholics, and on Presbyterians. The unlacing of these restrictions and the fight for religious equality was something which was to occupy the minds of the Guinness family into the nineteenth century. In 1690, though, what occupied William Read was how to make money from beer. It may have seemed like a convenient second income stream, and one which was compatible with farming.

Most of those licensed to sell beer also made it themselves, and Read could have grown his own barley, or arranged with a neighbour to supply it, knowing, or perhaps hoping, that he would find a ready market, even, as *Arthur's Round* suggests, selling to soldiers traipsing from one camp to the next, with Williamite and Jacobite coins equal in value. William Read had had a licence for eight years by the time his daughter Elizabeth was born, and she must have grown up with an understanding of both farming and of brewing, and of the commercial transactions which produced income from these activities. She brought this knowledge, and perhaps even the skill of brewing, to her marriage with a capable young land agent, Richard Guinness.

After a Dublin childhood, by 1722 Richard found himself in Celbridge in Kildare, barely five miles from Oughterard and the home of the Reads. He had a good job working as agent for the ambitious and prosperous Church of Ireland clergyman Dr Arthur Price. Dr Price was at that time Dean of Kildare (and was later to become Archbishop of Cashel) and busy completing a large and lovely house called Oakley Park in Celbridge. Proximity, at least, and presumably an introduction, brought Richard Guinness and Elizabeth Read together. They married, and in 1725, when Elizabeth Guinness was 27 years old, their first child was born. This event gives an insight into the strength of the relationship which must have existed between Dr Price and Richard Guinness, because the baby boy was named Arthur after his father's employer, who also stood as godfather.

Dr Price's Oakley Park was not the only fine new house locally. Just before the century turned, Bartholomew Van Homrigh, a Dutch Williamite merchant and Lord Mayor of Dublin, had built the house which would be called Celbridge Abbey, famous as the home of his daughter Esther. Esther, or 'Vanessa', had a love affair with the much older Jonathan Swift for many years, and it has been suggested that Arthur Price was himself an unsuccessful local suitor of Vanessa's.

In 1722, the year before Vanessa died, construction began on the winged Palladian mansion Castletown House, just beyond the town, built for William Conolly. Conolly was a Protestant lawyer from Donegal, the son of an innkeeper, and he profited hugely, and somewhat problematically, by buying up parcels of land forfeited by Catholics after the Williamite war; he was also elected to the Irish Parliament, and appointed Speaker of the House of Commons. His wife Katherine, born Conyngham, was not only socially more elevated than her husband, but also brought a couple of thousand pounds to the marriage, enabling him to begin to amass the enormous property portfolio which meant that, by the time he died, he was, certainly by reputation if not in fact, the richest man in Ireland.

Arthur Price was William Conolly's chaplain as well as his tenant in Celbridge, and Richard and Elizabeth Guinness were beneficiaries of this connection. Conolly told James Carbery to vacate a two-storey house in the main street for Price's use. This house was to form part of Richard Guinness's emolument, in that he and his small family were allowed to set up home there. And there they stayed, with Richard managing Price's property, even after Price himself had been appointed Bishop of Meath and moved to Ardbraccan in Navan.

This old malthouse in Celbridge was where Arthur Guinness grew up, near his father's employer's house, in the heart of the town, with commerce in his immediate vicinity, but surrounded by a mix of farmland and wooded countryside, and within striking distance of Dublin. There in Celbridge, the Conollys' superb Castletown was visible proof that social mobility was possible, and the Conollys' example showed that amassing great wealth, position and power did not have to mean abandoning friends of lesser status or turning your back on social justice. Katherine Conolly died in 1752 in her 90th year, having been 'drooping for some years', and Mary Delany, the late-in-life botanical artist whose vivid correspondence brings so much of eighteenth-century Ireland to life, wrote at the time that Mrs Conolly's table 'was open to all her friends of all ranks and her purse to the poor'. A century later an echo of this phrasing sounded in a letter from Arthur's son, also Arthur, to his own son Benjamin Lee, in response to news of the destitution across Ireland caused by the Famine. Anxious to find a way to help ease the suffering at home, Arthur Guinness II wrote: 'You know my dear Ben that my purse is open to the call.'

Fields of barley, grown for feed and malting, coloured the landscape around Celbridge golden brown and green, and would have been one of the most familiar views of Arthur's childhood. As he grew up and began to take more notice of his father's working life, Arthur would have witnessed his conduct of ongoing relationships with farmers in his role as land agent, and absorbed an understanding of agriculture, and particularly of the level of mental and physical labour demanded by a commitment to work the land fruitfully and turn a profit. The many breweries operating in Dublin alone represented an important market for farmers, not just for those in Celbridge and the rest of the rich farmland areas of Kildare, but also further afield. In later life Arthur's grasp of the economics and practicalities of farming life would serve him as he managed his supply chain, never forgetting that the quality of his brewing depended on the quality of his ingredients, whether drawn from storage or direct from the fields.

Arthur's first forays into brewing cannot be precisely pinpointed, tempting as it is to believe many of the stories. Did he learn brewing from his mother or maternal grandfather? Did Dr Price really brew 'black beer' at home and serve it at Ardbraccan dinners, as the Provost of Trinity College Dublin told it? Did Arthur make beer while working as a young man as a footman at Bishopscourt House, or while in Dr Price's employ? We know that Dr Price's death in 1752 led to Arthur being able to set up shop for the first time. Price's will contained the following bequests:

To servant, Richard Guinness, £100
To servant, Arthur Guinness, his son, £100.

Arthur's mother had died ten years earlier, at the age of 44, when the youngest of her six children was only 11, and Arthur, her eldest, was 17. Arthur, as the language of Price's will makes clear, had embarked on a career at his father's side, learning on the job, working for Price, getting to grips with land transactions, property law and a portfolio of leases, all while developing relationships with Catholic and Protestant tenants. By 27 he was skilled and experienced. He was also trusted and valued by his employer, as evidenced by the fact that father and son were each left the same sum, despite the fact that Richard Guinness had by then been working for Price for at least 30 years.

In the mid-eighteenth century, under usual circumstances at 27 a man was getting on a little. A boy might well have been apprenticed to learn a trade at 12 or 13, and while in the more elevated classes boys did not go to work until they had completed formal education, this happened relatively young. The life of a teenaged apprentice is perhaps uniquely recorded in the journal of John Tennent, apprenticed in 1786 for four years from the age of 14 to a Coleraine grocer. In passing, John's diary suggests that a man over 30 was far too old to be an attractive proposition to a woman: he noted with some disgust that his master was 'above thirty years of age yet he thinks that no woman would refuse to marry him'.

Dr Price had entered Trinity College Dublin at the age of 17, and had completed his degree by 21. At 26 he had already completed a readership and a curacy and had secured his first position as vicar. Arthur Guinness's inheritance came many years after Dr Price entered working life and some years before John Tennent did so, but these two examples nonetheless suggest that, in an age where childhood was abbreviated, the 27-year-old Arthur Guinness was at a relatively mature stage in his life by the time the crucial £100 came his way. The bequest enabled him to start planning a change in career.

Dr Price's death triggered a number of changes for the Guinness family. The time had now come for Richard to invest some of his savings in a family home, and he took over the sublease of a two-storey house in the main street of Celbridge. Richard had been a widower for ten years, and although now 62, an age so far past 30 that it would have seemed impossible to the youthful apprentice John Tennent, he married again. His new wife, and stepmother to his grown-up children, was Elizabeth Clare, the widowed landlady of the White Hart Inn, further along the main street. Arthur, out of employment now that Price was gone, began to work with his stepmother at the White Hart, and his career pivoted towards brewing.

Arthur was 31 when in 1755 he made his big move, deciding to combine his skill, ambition and £100 seed capital, and take the step of leasing a brewery. He had probably been saving and planning for some time, and it seems likely that his father helped him out with the initial investment. The brewery he chose was in Leixlip, only a few miles from Celbridge. Leixlip, like Celbridge, was close enough to Dublin that the city was accessible, not even ten miles away, yet also so prettily and rurally situated that Dubliners used it as a holiday destination. A London monthly, *The Universal Magazine of Knowledge and Pleasure*, ran a piece on it in October 1751, which found 'delicious country' around a 'charming retreat', approached by road with the river flowing 60 feet below.

Here, the magazine observed, 'numbers of polite people retire, during the summer, from the noise and hurry of the city'. It described the Salmon Leap Falls, which was a chief attraction, spanning the width of the river and tumbling 30 feet over rocks, with netted baskets fastened here and there to catch the leaping salmon. The waterfalls, the origin of the Norse name Leixlip (Salmon's Leap, Léim an Bhradáin), are unfortunately no longer visible, having been submerged when the river was dammed in 1947 by the Electricity Supply Board. James Pinny, who had recently moved from the Lyon Tavern in Capel Street in Dublin, set up afresh in Leixlip at the King's Arms. He advertised in *Pue's Occurrences* in 1757 not just 'the best accommodation' for 'Ladies and Gentlemen travelling', but also 'a large Ball Room, large enough for Twenty Couple to dance in', suggesting that the travellers who stayed at the King's Arms were not just passing through, but staying on to enjoy themselves.

By the time Arthur Guinness signed the lease on his new brewery in Leixlip, the magnificent Leixlip Castle, originally built in the twelfth century, was owned by William Conolly, though he wasn't living there. He had no need to, not when he could go home down the road to gorgeous Castletown. Instead, during

the 1750s, Leixlip Castle was home to George Stone, Church of
Ireland Archbishop of Armagh and Primate of All Ireland. Later,
the Lord Lieutenant, Lord Townshend, moved in. He and his wife
were described enthusiastically in a 1768 *Belfast News-Letter*
as being 'the life of Ireland', and when they retreated to Leixlip
Castle each summer it was for a round of concerts, entertainments and brilliant assemblies.

The life of Ireland, perhaps, but not Arthur Guinness's life.
At the brewery in Ralph Square, for Arthur, Leixlip's marvellous
scenery meant fields full of grain, the strength of the river meant
power for the mills, and the beautiful people escaping the noise
and hurry of town to stay at local inns and private houses meant
thirsty summer customers. The good road in and out could carry
beer west to Galway as well as into Dublin, so close it almost
counted as a local market. It was a well-supported, local start for
Arthur, commercially on his own for the first time, perfecting his
brewing and managing brewery and front of house.

Although Leixlip was to remain part of Arthur's life, not
just because of memories of his first brewery, but also because
of property investments he made there, the capital was calling.
Wanting to get established at the heart of Irish commercial life, he
moved his operation into the city in 1759. One younger brother
was already trading there, and a third brother would follow in
1760. Samuel, a couple of years younger than Arthur, had been
apprenticed to a goldbeater in London as a teenager, and returned
to Ireland around 1750 to set up shop in Dublin, at the sign of
the Hand and Hammer in Fishamble Street, which ran, and still
runs, from the east end of Christ Church Cathedral down to
Wood Quay on the river Liffey. As a goldbeater he made gold
leaf, which could then be used in bookbinding, decorative ecclesiastical work, furnishings and picture frames. Before long Samuel
moved eastward to Sycamore Alley (now Sycamore Street), only a
few minutes' walk away from Fishamble Street, but a little closer
to Dublin Castle and Trinity College. There had been a Quaker

meeting house in Sycamore Alley since the end of the seventeenth century, and the General Post Office was still there when Samuel Guinness moved his business in.

By 1760, Arthur and Samuel's younger brother Benjamin was also set up in Dublin, as a grocer in Werburgh Street, and there were Read relations living and working nearby as well: their uncle James had been a cutler in the city for many years, and a couple of Read cousins had been apprenticed to him. Thomas Read's landmark shop remains in the Read family's ownership, and is still trading in Parliament Street. Now carefully conserved and restored, House of Read is Dublin's oldest merchant house and shop.

Samuel Guinness's sign of the Hand and Hammer represented the act of beating gold into a thin sheet. Around Dublin there were countless illustrated commercial signs, essential in a city without universal literacy. A sign became a firm's address, as well as a way of navigating the city streets: newspapers of the late 1770s mentioned 'a Porter House, known by the sign of the Spread Eagle, Bride-street', a 'well-known House in Smock-alley, the Sign of the King's Arms', and 'the House known by the Sign of the Bear in Hoey's-court'. Every commercial street featured carved or painted signs, often double-sided and hanging perpendicular to the shopfront, so as to be easily visible to those approaching from either end of the street, and these signs must have contributed hugely to Dubliners' experience of moving around the built environment.

Taverns and inns, Arthur Guinness's future customers, were no exception to the rule of hanging out signs. If anything, their signs needed to work harder, not just to be familiar to regular customers, but so that they would be recognisably linked with refreshment for those new to the city, whether they were coming to stay or passing through. Mrs Swindle's chophouse, between the dilapidated Essex Bridge and the Custom House, was rather unappetisingly positioned at the Sign of the Old Sot's Hole. More neutrally named, perhaps, were other taverns like the Bear, and the Three Candlesticks, both in Smithfield, while the George and Dragon in Brown Street and the Red Lion in Bachelor's Walk showed English and Scottish influences.

Dublin was still characterised at this period by commercial and domestic buildings crammed cheek by jowl into narrow streets connected by alleys, lanes and courts. Just before Arthur's arrival in Dublin, an Act of Parliament established in 1757 the Commissioners for making Wide and Convenient Ways, Streets and Passages in the City of Dublin. His arrival coincided with this initiative to modernise and improve the built environment of the city, clearing away the central clusters of constricted medieval streets and laying out broader, airier, brighter spaces in which Dubliners could live and work. This work carried on for almost a hundred years, and resulted in, for example, the widening of Dame Street, and the streets which connected it to the river: D'Olier Street, Westmoreland Street and Parliament Street. Carlisle Bridge (now O'Connell Bridge) was also built, and Lower Sackville Street (now O'Connell Street) was extended to meet the bridge, making a wide artery connecting the north and south sides of the city.

Perhaps uniquely in urban development at this time, the streets were deliberately laid out to serve a commercial (specifically retail) purpose, while retaining both office space and residential accommodation in upper storeys. The laying out and building of the first of the city's Georgian garden squares, Rutland Square (now Parnell Square), was begun in the 1750s, and some of the city's landmark buildings began to appear, in the form of Bartholomew Mosse's pioneering Lying-In Hospital, now known as the Rotunda; Dublin Castle's Bedford Tower; and Leinster House, built for the Duke of Leinster and now in use by the Oireachtas, Ireland's parliament.

The city to which Arthur moved in 1759 had an eye on the future, on modernity, on progress. Trade was brisk, with agricultural produce central to the economy, and the property market was healthy. Dublin was growing both in footprint and in population, which would reach 200,000 by 1800. But there was of course more to the story than a thriving, expanding city of opportunity and healthy trade. Dublin was full of contradictions and polarities, a city of great wealth and great poverty, those in favour of union with Britain and those against it, Protestants and Catholics, the Gaelic Irish and the Ascendancy, the Viceroy and the Corporation of Dublin.

Dublin was divided into five distinct 'liberties': the archbishop's liberty, St Sepulchre with St Patrick's, St Nicholas Without and St Kevin's; Thomas Court, with Donore; St Patrick's; Christ Church, with Grangegorman; and Kilmainham. Each liberty had its local court system and administrative officers, and between them there was a predictable amount of jostling for position and jurisdiction. The bicameral Assembly of the Corporation of Dublin included representatives of the city guilds, the longest established of which were the merchants' and tailors' guilds, established in the twelfth and thirteenth century, respectively. Brewers and maltsters were members of the Guild of St Andrew, relatively recently established by a charter of 1696. The aldermen elected a Lord Mayor, who held office for a year; John Tew was the incumbent when Arthur came to Dublin.

This demonstrates the centrality of the commercial middle classes in civic life. Brewers were part of this, with membership of the guild making them eligible for a seat on the Corporation and a voice in civic administration. Up a notch on the social scale were those at the centre of government. Both the House of Lords and the House of Commons sat in the recently completed Parliament House, opposite the Front Gate of Trinity College on College Green, and those attached or adjacent to the governing élite basked in the glow of reflected status.

But the brewers and maltsters, and members of the other guilds, had perhaps more than anyone an active interest in the development and smooth running of the city. In hanging out their signs and establishing their businesses, they nailed their colours to the mast. They invested in Dublin. They needed the city to succeed, and were positioned to help it do so, not only by their contribution to the local and national economies, but also by their ready shouldering of civic duties and responsibilities.

When Arthur arrived, not entirely new to Dublin, but making a new relationship with it, the city still operated within a narrow medieval street structure, but plans were afoot to modernise and open up the streets. Street traders called through the city, summoning customers for their eggs, fresh fruit and vegetables, fish and shellfish, milk and whey, bringing to the city streets the colours and smells of rural and seaside lives. People came out from their houses and businesses when they heard the cry of the trader they needed, with knives to be sharpened, shoes and pots to be mended, old clothes and rags to be collected.

From the river, never too far away, came the calls of sailors and the sounds of boats and ships travelling up and down, and the smell of the river itself mingled with the salt sea air and the scents of turf and wood burning in hearths everywhere. More than 250 years later, for many Dubliners the smell of home would be the drifting early-morning scent of barley toasting in the Guinness brewery.

The Schedule to which the annexed Lease referrs

Three Marble Chimney Pieces
One Kitchen Greate Rack and Shelves
Two Small fixed Greates
Eleven Troughs
One float very bad
One Kieve very bad and two Brass Cocks
One Underback quite decayed
One Copper of Seventy Barrels with a large Brass Cock
Two Underback Pumps
Two old Coolers quite decayed
One Tunn
Six Oars
One Anke
One Horse Mill one Hopper and pair of Stones
Box of Drawers and Desk in the Office
The thirty first of December 1759 Nine

Schedule attached to the 1759 lease of the St James's Gate brewery.

TWO

OPENING THE GATE

If the newspaper *Pue's Occurrences* formed part of Arthur Guinness's news sources during his Leixlip years, he might well have seen the old brewery at St James's Gate in Dublin advertised there in 1756, and been mulling over for some time the notion of taking it on, before finally committing to it in 1759. The advertisement described it simply as a 'Dwelling House, Malt House, and large Brewery in St Thomas Street near St James's Gate, formerly in the Occupation of Paul Espiness'. Paul Espinasse (as the name more usually appears) was a Huguenot brewer who had leased the brewery from Mark Rainsford, and had died in 1750. The brewery had therefore been on the market for several years, suggesting that it cannot have been a particularly attractive proposition. At any rate, a few enquiries would have satisfied Arthur that there was no immediate pressure to act. He was busy with the Leixlip premises, building up his business, setting money aside, and quite possibly enlisting his father's help.

By 1759 he was ready, and no one else had stepped in to take up the brewery at St James's Gate. He signed the lease, which survives, and describes in full colour Arthur's new property:

> a commodious dwelling house with a large pleasure garden and fish pond, the brewery with copper kieve and Mill, two large malt houses, stabling for 12 horses, with loft to hold 200 loads of hay, and an uninterrupted supply of water free from tax or pipe money, all in complete order ready for business.

The site was set up on the hill beside St James's Church, a five-minute walk downhill to the river Liffey. The lease was for 9,000 years, at an annual rent of £45, with a nominal premium to satisfy the requirements of contract law. The place had lain idle for a decade, and was hardly shipshape, despite being described as ready for business. The lease does clarify the state of some of the equipment:

> One Kieve very bad and two Brass Cocks; One under-bank quite decayed; One Copper; seventy Barrels with a large brass Cock; Two Underbank pumps; Two old Coolers quite decayed.

If a copper kieve, which was a kind of vat, had been left unused for ten years it would have required some serious attention, if not replacement. Even if the buildings had been left in good order originally, they must have suffered in the way all unoccupied premises do. Arthur, in calculating his finances, had to allow not just for the initial payment, but for remedial works to get the brewery to operational standard. On top of that he would have needed to reserve some capital for buying ingredients, finding and paying workers, and making his own move from living in Leixlip to living in the house at St James's Gate. The Leixlip brewery he left in his brother's hands.

St James's Gate is reputed to have been the western entry point, and toll point, of the medieval walled city of Dublin, although archaeological and documentary evidence instead suggests that it was in fact a much later street gate between the parishes of St Catherine's and St James's. According to the historian Bernadette Cunningham, the gate between Thomas Street and James's Street was probably known as St James's Gate simply because it was the access point between the city of Dublin and the suburban parish of St James.

Other stories about the area have been told and retold until they almost take on the texture of fact. An old favourite is that for over 800 years Christian pilgrims set off on the hazardous journey from the holy well near St James's Gate to join the well-known Camino de Santiago, making for the twelfth-century cathedral of Santiago de Compostela in Galicia in northern Spain, where St James is said to be buried. Here pilgrim routes from all over Europe converged, with people walking the path not just to visit the apostle's burial place, but to earn indulgences, remission of punishment for sin.

It's a seductive idea, that Irish pilgrims gathered in Dublin, at St James's Well beside St James's Gate, and set off from there to merge with other European tributaries, and move towards the shrine at Santiago. Seductive, but deceptive. Bernadette Cunningham, who has studied the travels of Irish pilgrims between the twelfth and fifteenth centuries, and the area around St James's Gate, reported 'neither documentary evidence nor historical logic' to support the idea, which 'makes no sense historically or geographically'. However, there is certainly a link now, and the sacristy of St James's Church is one of the places where modern pilgrims can get their *credencial*, the pilgrim passport. The scallop shell, closely associated with the Spanish route, the Camino de Santiago, and with St James himself, forms part of the present-day logo of St James's Hospital in Dublin.

Around the feast of St James, 25 July, a fair was held, 'fast by the Well'. The Corporation of Dublin abolished it in 1738 but somehow it was revived. Walter Thomas Meyler, born in 1813, described it as he remembered it from his early youth, with its 'ranges of stands covered with baskets of cherries, gooseberries, gilt gingerbread, toys, tin whistles, drums, tops, horses, and whips, and the decorated figure of St. Patrick'. For the small boy, it was his 'gala day of the year', and any coins that came his way he put by so as to have spending money for the fair.

People streamed into James's Street, which was filled with temporary market stalls and ale stalls. Rather too many ale stalls, in some people's view. People drank and mucked about at the Dublin fairs, and while the occasions may have been exciting and colourful for children, they did come in for their share of criticism as disruptive and anti-social. In the early seventeenth century, Barnaby Rich, who tended towards the scathing when it came to everything Irish, wrote in his 1610 *New Description of Ireland* of his disgust at St James's Fair:

> The commoditie that is there to be vented, is nothing else but Ale, no other merchandize but only Ale: I thinke such another Faire was never heard of in any other place, where a man can not buy so much as a penniworth of pins, but what money hee hath to bestow, hee must lay it out for Ale, and yet it carries the name of S. James his faire.

St James's was not the only fair reviled for its overly raucous entertainments and overindulgence in ale. The Donnybrook Fair, held for a fortnight in high summer, was notorious in the main for its drunkenness and fighting, rather than for its stalls and tents. Each August the newspapers wearily reported incidents of violence, debauchery and riotous behaviour, and of drunken people staggering back into the city afterwards, often assaulting one another and passers-by as they went.

Members of various criminal gangs could get enormously wound up at the fair, leading to serious violence. The Liberty Boys, a gang of tailors and weavers from the Coombe, and the Ormond Boys, a gang of butchers from Ormond Market on Ormond Quay, detested one another, and in 1752 one newspaper reported that members of the two factions on their way home from the fair:

bred much Confusion in the Streets which they passed thro', knocking down and cutting one another in a most inhuman Manner, three of whom are killed, besides many innocent People maimed.

The Donnybrook Fair was a thorn in the side of the Corporation of Dublin. It often opened several days early and closed several late, ignoring the terms of its licence, and in 1773 a frustrated Lord Mayor, accompanied by sheriffs, went out to Donnybrook and had all the tents taken down. In 1777 a woman was murdered. In 1778 one man suffered a fractured skull and another a broken leg during a fracas. Businesspeople objected to the fairs not just because of the chaotic behaviour around them, but because of their loss of trade. Between the Palmerstown and Donnybrook fairs, this loss was estimated by the *Dublin Evening Post* in 1779 at £20,000 annually.

For Arthur Guinness, St James's Fair was of specific local interest, happening as it did on his new doorstep. Brewers in general had several reasons to object to the fairs, including the loss of trade (even if it didn't quite reach the level estimated), the effects on anti-social behaviour around the city and the ammunition they provided to those opposed to alcohol. Barnaby Rich had referred to 'ale' as the principal evil at the St James's Fair, but the distinction between ale and beer was gradually becoming blurred.

Hops had first arrived from Flanders in the early sixteenth century, and their inclusion in the brewing process of ale resulted in beer. Beer had a sharper taste after the addition of hops, and it also kept better and longer than ale, because of the antibiotic properties of the hops. So while ale had to be drunk fairly quickly after being brewed, and was therefore suited to being drunk in the house in which it had been made, the new beer could be sold commercially. By the seventeenth century everyone was using hops, and the terms ale and beer became interchangeable.

Brown ale, also known as brown beer, and sometimes brown stout, also developed around the seventeenth century, and was the product of a change in the malt-curing process which gave the drink a deeper colour. English duties on beer and malt, the steeped and germinated barley grain, led to a higher and higher hop content. This changed the taste of the drink so dramatically that people began to mix it with ale to keep it palatable. In this 'half-and-half', as economic historian Oliver MacDonagh put it, 'the beer masked the deficiencies of the ale. The ale moderated both the expense and the acidity of the beer.'

Ultimately these developments led to the production of a hop-heavy dark beer which not only had a long travelling and shelf life but actually improved for not being drunk immediately, and moreover was cheaper to make. This beer was porter, which would one day be at the heart of Arthur Guinness's success. However, it was also porter that turned Ireland from a net exporter of beer in the early eighteenth century to a net importer from 1741 on.

Arthur was expanding his business within an industry in decline. He had taken on a disused, out-of-repair brewery in a city in which he had never lived or worked. Irish barley production had faltered during the crop failures of the early 1740s, and the reduction of tithes on pasture was causing farmers to turn away from tillage to dairy.

These were the negatives, but Arthur had plenty in the positive column. He had several years of experience, not just of brewing but of running a brewery, and of financial management. The lengthy lease on the brewery promised stability, and though he was new to Dublin he had an extended family network *in situ*, and a father who was still active and in a position to advise, perhaps even to help out financially. Arthur wanted to master the brewing process sufficiently to make a reliable beer, consistently good but also affordable. He planned to sell his beer to the owners of licensed premises, who would no longer have to brew their own and would therefore be able to concentrate on their front of house and on any additional strands to their business, such as accommodation.

Although Dublin was still a small city, its growing population was already served by about a hundred breweries and distilleries. Alcohol was part not just of domestic life but of life through the city. Dr John Rutty recorded 3,500 drinking venues in Dublin in 1749, when the city had about 150,000 inhabitants. The anti-alcohol public discourse, and ultimately the temperance movement which was still to come in the 1820s, was focused on spirits in general, and whiskey in particular, rather than beer. Beer, as we have already seen, was treated more as a thirst-quencher and a source of nutrition than as a means to get drunk.

Arthur's mind was not solely occupied with business, for he became engaged to Olivia Whitmore. She was the daughter of William Whitmore, whom the *Dublin Evening Post* later described as an 'eminent grocer' in Essex Street, and Mary Grattan, from a landowning family in Kildare. They were married in June 1761, when she had just turned 19 and Arthur was 35. Olivia brought to the marriage a dowry of £1,000: ten times the value of the £100 bequest from Dr Price which was Arthur's seed capital. She therefore offered a useful financial cushion for Arthur, as he carefully managed his outgoings against his income.

Olivia, my great-great-great-great-great-grandmother, is perhaps known more for her role as a mother than anything else, particularly because she was the mother of three sons who succeeded Arthur at the brewery. But there was of course more to her than childbearing and her dowry. Olivia was not the pampered child of moneyed gentry. She was the daughter of a merchant operating his grocery business in Essex Street in the centre of the city, about a mile east of St James's Gate.

Olivia grew up familiar with the pressures and compromises, the struggles and successes which were part of running a business, and brought this knowledge to her marriage as well.

Like any business owner, Arthur must always have carried work issues in his head, never fully switching off at home or in the company of others. Even if Olivia did not actively advise Arthur, she could listen and understand when he was wrestling with a problem or weighing up a decision. Socially, the Whitmores were more elevated than the Guinnesses, and so his in-laws would have boosted Arthur's position, and may also have made commercial introductions, although they were not in the brewing business.

The marriage of Arthur and Olivia Guinness was a long one and seems to have been happy. It was certainly fruitful: in 1790, Arthur wrote of the 'Ten Children now living out of one & twenty born to us, & more likely yet to come'. In fact no more children were born to the couple, despite Arthur's desire. However much he, and perhaps both of them, wanted to keep enlarging their family, 21 pregnancies and births in 29 years was an enormous strain on a woman's body, and Olivia was already fortunate to have survived that many. Her age – she was 48 at the time Arthur wrote of his expectation of more children – meant that further pregnancies, even if possible, would have represented a greater risk. The loss of a child at birth or in infancy was common, but that did not mean it was not devastating when it happened – and the couple had lost 11.

Bartholomew Mosse, a surgeon whose wife and son had died in the aftermath of childbirth, founded the Rotunda Lying-In Hospital in Dublin in 1745, thought to be the first hospital of its kind in the world. But it started with only ten beds, so it is much more likely that Olivia Guinness gave birth at home than in the new hospital. Although there was no formalised midwifery training, there were women working as midwives, and indeed one of Olivia's father's neighbours in Essex Street, Mary Byrne, was one. When the time came for an expectant mother to deliver, practical assistance during the birth itself was given by the midwife, if there was one available locally, and whichever female relatives lived with or near her. Friends and neighbours rallied round for the lying-in period.

The length of the lying-in period varied not only according to how healthy and fit the new mother was, but also according to how much money and household help there was available. Over the 29 years of Olivia's pregnancies and births, the Guinnesses' economic and domestic situation improved and improved, and it seems likely that after every birth she would have been able to take the time and rest necessary to recover. There is no evidence of how she fed her babies. Better-off families did tend to employ wet nurses. A newspaper advertisement in 1784 ran:

> A Wet Nurse Wanted. Wanted to Nurse within Doors, a healthy young Woman, with a full Breast of Milk, not more than two Months old. Such a Person, every Way qualified, will hear of an eligible Situation by inquiring at No. 45, Strand-street, within one Door of Capel-street.

If the Guinnesses did employ a wet nurse, and Olivia did not therefore breastfeed her children, the resumption of her ovulation would have been faster, making the next pregnancy more likely to come hard on the heels of the last. In an act of love of family and of home, Arthur ensured that those of his children who did not survive were brought out of the city and home to Kildare, to Oughterard Hill, to be buried near their grandparents and great-grandparents.

The 'commodious dwelling house with a large pleasure garden and fish pond' within the brewery compound was not to be the Guinness family's only home. In 1764 the as yet small family acquired Beaumont House near Artane, a relatively plain but spacious house about five miles north-east of St James's Gate. The difference in atmosphere was significant, from an industrial city-centre site to what was then a rural setting, the house surrounded by fields and approached along a long tree-lined avenue. Although

Arthur Guinness may not have written the description himself, he presumably approved the text of the advertisement for Beaumont he placed in *Saunders's News-Letter* in 1775:

> To be let for a Term of Years or Lives, or the Interest to be sold, BEAUMONT, near Artain, with any Quantity of Meadow Ground from 20 to 53 Acres, the House, Garden, and Offices new and in excellent Order; the Situation delightful, having a View of the Sea, City of Dublin, Wicklow Mountains, &c. Also to be let, a Tenement and Garden in the Town of Glasnevin. Inquire of Mr. Guinness, at James's gate.

It reads like a perfect place to make a family home, with plenty of meadowland and a garden, as well as a house and offices in good shape. From here Arthur and Olivia could see Dublin Bay and look south to the mountains, but could also look over the city towards the brewery and work. Beaumont seems to have been advertised as a summer let, and later descriptions include references to a hothouse, stables, a coach house and a dairy, as well as 'keeping for one or two cows'.

Arthur moved his family life away from the heart of the city, but he made sure to keep his connections there strong. Essential to his position as a brewer and a businessman was membership of the relevant trade guild, which in his case was St Andrew's, the Brewers and Maltsters. Some of the guilds, like the Shoemakers and the Merchant Tailors, had received their charters in the early fifteenth century, but St Andrew's was relatively new, having had its charter only since 1696.

When Arthur was a child in Celbridge the guild held its meetings in Hoey's Court, sitting between Werburgh Street and Dublin Castle, and now usually remarked on for being in 1667 the birthplace of Jonathan Swift. The Guild of Glovers also had a hall in Hoey's Court, and the Goldsmiths met in Werburgh Street.

The Brewers moved to Keyzar's Lane off Cornmarket, then to Tailors' Hall in Back Lane; from the early nineteenth century they would move east into an entirely different district and meet in Morrison's Hotel at the corner of Dawson Street and Nassau Street, overlooking Trinity College.

Arthur set his application to join the guild in motion as soon as possible, and in fact was admitted eight months before the St James's Gate lease was signed. On 24 April 1759, his application was considered by the the Master, Warden and Brethren of the guild:

> the Petition of Arthur Guinness being read praying to be admitted into the franchises & Lybertys of this Corporation, he was accordingly admitted on paying a fine of two Guineas.

This was signed by those present. All except the Master, James Taylor, finished their signatures with elaborately repeating loops and twirling flourishes, which contextualise Arthur's now-famous calligraphy. Two months later, at the June meeting, Thomas Williams and Arthur Guinness were sworn 'free Brothers'. In August, when the minutes of the meeting were complete, they were passed to Arthur, and he added his signature to the rest on the page, lastly but beautifully. That December, he was already moving up the page, with more newly sworn Brothers below him; two years later, in December 1761, he was elected Warden, and in September 1766 Master.

As Warden, one of his first responsibilities was to serve on a committee to consider how best to prevent the 'immoderate Drinking of raw spirits by the lower Class of People in & about the City of Dublin to the great Detriment of this Corporation & Destructive of our Industrious Manufacturers'. It was essential that the brewers were not tainted by public anxieties about drinking alcohol, which were trained on the 'lower Class of People'. In typical public discourse, like the reaction to the fairs, alcohol was blamed for poverty, violence and uncontrolled behaviour. There were plenty of other contexts in which alcohol was a commonplace and uncontentious element of people's lives.

Alcohol was a traditional offering in hospitality. It was the companion to food, the mark of celebration, used to drink the monarch's health or toast a departing emigrant. It was regarded as medicinal. In the form of beer it was considered both nutritious and thirst-quenching, and in the form of wine it played its part in both Catholic and Protestant church services. Brewing and distilling were traditional activities in monastic life. But whiskey-drinking in particular was on the rise by the late eighteenth century, and while the temperance movement had yet to swing into action, for those public commentators who identified problematic drinkers as spirit drinkers, beer seemed a plausible alternative. The Brewers' and Maltsters' Guild, represented by Arthur Guinness and the rest of the committee, could most heartily agree with this.

Guild membership was important not just for commercial life but also for politics, because the trade guilds sent forward representatives to the Dublin City Assembly, the governing body of Dublin Corporation. The Upper House of the Assembly was made up of the Lord Mayor and 24 aldermen, and the Common Council, the lower house, was made up of 96 guild representatives and 48 sheriffs' peers. Arthur would go on to be elected a guild representative. These were elected for a term of three years, while the aldermen and sheriffs served for life and also acted as magistrates.

Action areas generally concerned public projects such as street paving and lighting, maintenance of the harbour, bridges, drainage and sewerage, and to discuss and budget for these, the Assembly met quarterly at the Tholsel, a multipurposed civic building in Skinner's Row. One of the Tholsel's functions was as a courthouse, and the Quarter Sessions, precursor to the circuit court, were held there. The building was so dilapidated and unfit for purpose that eventually a hole in the floor enabled prisoners held in the room beneath it to escape. The Assembly moved in 1804 to South William Street, to a building formerly occupied by the Society of Artists in Ireland, still known today as City Assembly House.

Arthur was a planner, putting forethought into every move, and it must have been satisfying to see the results as the component parts of his commercial, family and civic life slipped into place one by one. Occasionally something didn't work out entirely as planned and by 1764 it became obvious that one of those things was the brewery's water supply. A clause in the St James's Gate lease purported to convey the interest in the premises to Arthur,

> together with the full and free use Liberty and privi-
> lidge of the said Pipe water or City Water Course Lying
> on the west of the premises gratis and without any
> Consideration to be paid for the same.

It was Arthur's responsibility, or his lawyer's, before signing the lease, to interrogate whether or not the promise of free water was one which could actually be made: the principle of *caveat emptor*, let the buyer beware, applied to the purchase. The Corporation of Dublin was certainly of the view that no such undertaking should have been given, and that the new lessor had no business relying on it. The brewery tenant was not entitled to a free water supply at the city's expense, and Arthur would have to pay. A Corporation committee overseeing the pipe water had used 'all reasonable methods', it reported,

> to induce Mr. Guinness to become tenant to the city for
> water, which he has hitherto declined, insisting upon a
> right thereto, without paying any compensation for the
> same … We therefore think it would be proper, that the

committee be empowered to take such effectual methods
as may be necessary to prevent his having any future
supply of water, until he agrees to pay for the same and
discharge the arrears.

This was fighting talk, but Arthur had no intention of backing
down, and the argument was to grind on for years. There were
episodes of high drama, including the time in 1775 that Arthur
deliberately widened the culvert allowing water into the brewery;
when the Corporation sent a crew to fill the culvert, Arthur
himself took a pickaxe from one of the labourers and brandished
it while using 'very much improper language', then

stood with the pickaxe in their way and prevented them
and declared, that if they filled it up from end to end, he
would immediately open it.

This scene is all the more extraordinary for being described in
the Calendar of the Ancient Records of Dublin. This contains the
minutes of all the meetings of the City Assembly. Arthur, now a
member of the Common Council of Assembly, attended the meetings. At an earlier meeting in 1775, he had been selected from
the Common Council as one of the committee of directors of the
Ballast Office which oversaw Dublin's docks. On the one hand
the Corporation entrusted him as a citizen and a guild representative to take on this kind of responsibility, while on the other
it found itself in an adversarial engagement with him. It gives
an insight into Arthur's character that he was not so intent on
becoming part of the establishment, making the right connections
and joining the right organisations, that he did not prioritise the
interests of his business.

It was not the case that he wanted to fit in at any cost: the
promise of free water held out in the lease might have been made
in error, but the water supply was so essential to the brewery that

Arthur simply had to secure it. In 1784 he did so. It involved Arthur's taking out an injunction against the Lord Mayor, and showing his preparedness to engage in a legal wrangle for as long as it took, but that year, 25 years after signing the brewery lease, he was given a lease on the water for 8,975 years. It was a victory for tenacity and for Arthur.

Irish postage stamp, 1959.

THREE

DIPPING AND RISING

The new brewery was fully operational and the water was now at least on its way to being secured. Rising beer sales through the later 1750s must have seemed marvellously promising to Arthur, but a slump in the beer trade – consumption, sales and revenue – hit from 1762 to 1773. Nationally, consumption dropped a full third, from 600,000 barrels to 400,000. In the meantime, the number of barrels of porter coming into the country was going in the other direction, from nearly 30,000 to nearly 60,000 barrels. The taxation system favoured imported British beer over Irish, with Irish brewers paying 5s 6d on a 40-gallon barrel of ale, while British brewers paid just 1s 3d on the same.

There was no competition in the hop market. Ireland was only permitted to import British hops, and struggled to grow her own. In Dublin, brewers were closing breweries, unable to bridge the gap between the cost of making beer and the difficulty in selling it. This was tricky timing, given Arthur's commercial investment, now overlaid by his domestic commitments to his new wife and rapidly increasing young family. He must have wracked his brains night after night over how to respond to the change in market conditions.

Porter was initially attractive to customers solely because of its low cost, but palates adjusted and appetites awakened. An Irish taste for porter began to develop. Long before Arthur Guinness had come to Dublin, Irish brewers had begun experimenting with brewing this hoppy, dark, London concoction, and Faulkner's *Dublin Journal* had in 1740 remarked on how much better the quality of Dublin-brewed porter was than the London import, how superior it was 'in strength, colour, and taste'. The newspaper reported that the Dublin version was available in pubs in Weavers Square, the Coombe, Bride Street, Castle Street, Francis Street and Dame Street, all within a mile of St James's Gate. In 1757, a couple of years before Arthur signed the lease on the Dublin brewery, the Dublin Society (later the Royal Dublin Society), ever ready with incentives and encouragements, had offered a prize for 'the most and best Beer, brewed in Imitation of Porter; a Sample to be produced before the Society'. Yet by the late 1770s there were still only three breweries in Dublin making porter.

In 1773 a Parliamentary Committee was established in response to lobbying from the increasingly frustrated Irish breweries. This was the brewers' great opportunity to put their case persuasively, and first up in front of the committee was George Thwaites, the then Master of the Corporation of Brewers, and a brewer of 34 years' standing. He was well prepared, with his facts and arguments marshalled, and he was articulate in giving evidence to the committee that the trade had suffered badly, particularly over the previous seven years. He ascribed the difficulties, in part, to the increased costs of hops, malt, fuel and labour. The high cost of ingredients had to be offset by using less of each, which ruined the quality of the final product.

Recouping expenses by hiking up the price paid by the customer wasn't an option: if anything, he pointed out, the Irish brewers needed to drop their prices to be competitive in the face of the cheaper and increasingly popular English porter. If they raised the price of their ale at all, the publicans would sell nothing but porter, 'and the whole Trade of Brewing in Dublin and consequently the Revenue arising from it would fall to the Ground'. Joseph Andrews, a 'considerable brewer', said the situation was so bad that he had been seriously considering setting up business in Holyhead and shipping his beer back into Dublin.

The third and last man examined was Arthur Guinness, also described as a 'considerable brewer', who said more or less the same thing. He had now been brewing at St James's Gate for 14 years, but reported having travelled to Wales on a reconnoitre of Caernarvon and Holyhead. He hadn't found an available existing brewery there, but 'he would at this Day settle there, and build a Brewery, if he could be assured that the Laws would stand as they are, for Seven Years'. He didn't want to go to all the trouble and expense of setting up from scratch if there was any chance of reform, which would leave him stranded in Wales, having expended capital and energy, only to be left without any of the intended financial advantages of being there.

The brewers had done their best, but from a parliamentary point of view it wasn't convincing enough to precipitate the longed-for shift. Almost nothing had changed four years later. In 1777, when the Provost of Trinity, John Hely-Hutchinson, wrote of the 'poisonous forces' deliberately hamstringing Ireland:

> Beer they export to us in such quantities as almost to ruin our brewery; but they prevent our exportation to them by duties, laid on the import there, equal to a prohibition. Of malt they make large exports to us, to the prejudice of our agriculture, but have absolutely prohibited our exportation of that commodity to them. Some manufactures they retain solely to themselves, which we are prohibited from exporting, and cannot import from any country but Great Britain, as glass of all kinds. Hops they do not allow us to import from any other place, and in a facetious style of interdiction, pronounce such importation to be a common nuisance.

As the brewers' combined efforts to change policy foundered, it seemed as if Arthur's meticulously planned and financed move to Dublin was running into structural barbed wire. But there was one more route to try. At the pub counters, it was porter that was spoiling things for the Dublin brewers. When it came to price, preference and prevalence they couldn't compete. If Dubliners wanted porter and bought porter, Arthur would be the one to give it to them. He could be as nimble as his business required him to be, and so in 1778, at the age of 53, he began to sell porter. To sell in 1778 he must have begun brewing in 1777.

Arthur was not the only Irish brewer to turn to porter. Newspaper advertisements around this time hum with the promise of Irish porter as the coming drink, just as good as the London kind, something everyone in the trade was agreed was a good choice, something that would benefit the country. Farrell's brewery in Blackpitts was an early porter producer, and was believed by the Purser family, three generations of whom would work at Arthur Guinness and Sons, to have been the first.

In 1776, John Purser, an experienced porter brewer, came to Dublin from London, to take a job at Farrell's, where he put his porter-brewing skills to use. His descendants would prove essential to the success of the Guinness brewery. His eldest son John Purser Senior entered Arthur's service in 1799 as a bookkeeper, and became a partner in 1820; his grandson John Purser Junior entered as an apprentice brewer, also in 1799; and his great-grandson John Tertius Purser became head brewer, eventually declining a partnership and retiring in 1886, when the company was floated.

But in the late eighteenth century Dublin breweries were still just experimenting with porter. In 1779 an empty brewery in the Coombe was advertised to let, as 'particularly well situated for brewing Porter, being very roomy and extensive'. Patrick Sweetman made a porter in his brewery at 81 St Stephen's Green (which much later would form part of the Guinness family home), advertised as, 'equal to any Porter imported into this Kingdom'. This was the first the public had heard of it, because Sweetman had 'hitherto declined advertising it for Sale, until Age should have brought it to proper Maturity'. He had brewed it 'neither too strong nor too thin', and he was now selling it for £3 for a hogshead, with a deposit return scheme of ten shillings on his own hogsheads.

In a further advertisement in 1779, Sweetman remarked on 'the almost general Wish of the Publicans of this City to retail Irish Porter'. Alderman Warren of Mill Street, not shy about using his status as a member of the Corporation of Dublin to promote his business, advertised his Plain Porter, and finished with a persuasive bit of copywriting stating that 'a Preference given to their own Brewery will be productive of the greatest Utility, and an immediate Advantage to the Nation in general'. Robert Pettit, in Spring Garden Lane off Dame Street, stated at the end of 1779 that his was the 'first house opened for sale of Irish Brown Stout Porter in this City'.

So Arthur may not have been the first off the blocks, but rather was part of an excited urban revolution towards what might easily have ended up being called the brown stuff. The brewing lobby continued to exert pressure and seek support, and indeed found it in Henry Grattan, an MP and barrister who was also a relative of Olivia Guinness. He succeeded in having further import duties imposed in 1789 and 1791. This did encourage Irish beer production, but the die was already cast as far as porter was concerned. Dublin had a taste for it.

At home, the first of Arthur's children were now old enough to look beyond Beaumont and the brewery. For Hosea, the eldest, born in 1765, this meant first Winchester College in 1777, then Oxford University. A useful fee discount was available for both, because Hosea qualified as Founder's Kin through an ancestral connection of Olivia's with William of Wykeham, founder of Winchester and New College, Oxford. Hosea came home to Trinity College Dublin for his doctorate in divinity and then took holy orders.

The next brother down was another Arthur, born in 1768, but rather than decamping to Winchester, he went to the English Grammar School run by Samuel Whyte at 75 Grafton Street, a school later described by Thomas Moore, a past pupil who later became known as Ireland's national bard, as 'the best then in Dublin'. Just before Christmas each year Whyte's boys (or 'Gentlemen') underwent what sounds like a terrifying process of examination, held in public 'in presence of a crowded Audience of Ladies and Gentlemen, Parents and Friends of the young Gentlemen Candidates'. Every pupil was issued with 12 tickets, and was then questioned in front of this audience of their family, friends and teachers. If a boy couldn't answer a question correctly, he returned a ticket, and whoever had the most tickets at the end was awarded the prize.

It seems possible that Arthur II, who would then have been about 15, was the 'Guinness' who is recorded as having run the gauntlet in 1783, and carried off the following: Grammar and Use of Globes, second division premium; Reading, fourth class premium certificate; Writing, third division certificate. Samuel Whyte, the founder and principal of the school, used the *Hibernian Journal* to explain the difference in awards:

> As many of the Candidates appeared with equal advantage, and cut for the Premium in their respective Classes, they got Premium Certificates to distinguish them from those who were entitled to Certificate only, having missed only one or not more than three Questions.

If this was young Arthur, then he was not only good at his lessons but also unruffled enough to be able to acquit himself well in front of an audience. The school, founded in 1758, had very quickly developed an excellent reputation, and it was alma mater not just to Thomas Moore and Arthur Guinness but to Arthur Wellesley, the Duke of Wellington, and Robert Emmet. Today it is home to the latest incarnation of Bewley's Café, whose buns and coffee would have seemed like a fabulous treat for the eighteenth-century schoolboys.

Arthur's next son, Edward (born in 1772), became a lawyer, but Benjamin (born in 1777) and William Lunell (born in 1779) would both go on to be brewers, as would young Arthur, who entered the brewery from school, skipping the university step which may have seemed irrelevant with a business to learn. Arthur had such a large family, and it was stretched over so many years, that his eldest, Hosea, was no longer living at home and porter had come into play at the brewery before William Lunell was even born. It must have been both reassuring and gratifying for Arthur to realise that, of his numerous capable children, three had the inclination to carry on the business, and even more reassuring and gratifying when they formally entered the business, and it became Arthur Guinness and Son.

Family mattered. In the only surviving letter in Arthur's handwriting, written in 1790, he wrote of his investment of between four and five thousand pounds in building flour mills and three thousand pounds in getting the milling business started. His family needed him to make money for them to live on, but were coming into their own as adults:

> The great increase of my Family required every exertion
> of mine to make this great extension of my Business, in
> addition to my Brewery which is still extending.

George Martelli, whose biography of the first Earl of Iveagh my great-grandfather commissioned, wrote that 'even in Ireland' the eighteenth century was an age of scepticism and tolerance. The rising merchant class, Arthur's milieu, was concerned less by religion (except when it came to morality) and politics (except for the national question, and tariffs on beer) than by making the best of their lives and providing for their families, not just materially but also when it came to education and opportunity. The general imperative was to obey 'the laws of sobriety, frugality, thrift and industry, which were not only pleasing to the Deity but also best calculated to advance a man in the world'. Arthur cared about and for his family, adhered to his Protestant faith and lived by the principles of public duty and charity. Although the brewery did fairly well for Arthur, in his day it was largely a local business, supplying within Dublin.

It wasn't until 1820 that a broader Irish and English market opened up, and not until the 1860s that full-blown exporting began. The huge profits and wealth that the brewery would one day generate could hardly have been imaginable in 1790, when Arthur found himself in the embarrassing situation of apologising for not having paid one sum of money because he had not yet recovered another sum owed to him from another source, in the familiar, careful choreography of managing cash flow. While he did not have the same means as later Guinnesses might have done, he still gave generously of his time, his experience and his money.

In his Leixlip days, Arthur had become a member of the Kildare Knot, and rose to become its secretary and president. The Kildare Knot was one of a number of branches of the Friendly Brothers of St Patrick. The aim of the Friendly Brothers, for 'Noblemen and Gentlemen', was to 'promote public and private Virtue', which they did by modelling brotherly love, donating to charity and getting up public monuments. Fortunately, meeting in taverns was not incompatible with virtue, and in the 1750s the Friendly Brothers met in the Rose Tavern in Essex Street, only a mile or so from St James's Gate.

The Brothers publicly adopted moral standpoints and made resolutions of joint actions. In 1784 they declared that, because the 'present calamitous State of the Manufacturers of this Kingdom calls loudly for assistance', their brethren would 'not from this Date hereof Purchase for or consume by themselves or their Families, any other than the Manufactures of this their Native Country': they would buy Irish, and only Irish.

The Brothers' founding principle was a shared opposition to duelling. The practice, which astonishingly continued in Ireland up to 1841, was part of the old code of chivalry, and involved a scheduled combat between two people, evenly matched in their weapons, and with no additional advantage on either side – no one duelled with the sun in their eyes, or having to fight uphill. The practice was supposed to result in 'satisfaction' for the party whose injured honour had sparked the match, but inevitably people were killed.

Famously, Daniel O'Connell killed John d'Esterre in a duel in 1815, thought to have taken place to the west of the Reads' and Guinnesses' graves in Oughterard, but O'Connell was a reluctant participant, and subsequently refused to duel again, unable to square the practice with his Catholic morality. The masculine ritual of duelling somehow clung on through the Enlightenment, remained largely outside the law, and maintained its deep connection with honour, despite the fact that it frequently ended with one person unlawfully killing another, usually in a public place, to settle a score which might have turned on no more than an insult. The Kildare Knot, its fellow Knots around the country (and by the early nineteenth century in English cities like London and Bath), and its parent body, the Friendly Brothers, were totally opposed to duelling.

The Kildare Knot was more than a fraternal dining club, or a social network, though these aspects of it were also important to Arthur. Membership was also a declaration of adherence to a particular moral code. Anyone who met Arthur for the first time and heard that he was a member would understand what it meant about his character and his intentions. It would enable them to place him. Arthur's Christianity was important to him, and when considering what this really meant in his day-to-day life, it is worth thinking about how Patrick Guinness distinguishes between the practical impulses of the two main Christian churches in Ireland by the late eighteenth century: he observes that, for Catholics, 'devotional faith was now much more remarkable', while for

> literate and commercial Protestants ... faith was not so important, but good works were now the best practical everyday means of demonstrating a desire to help humanity.

This idea was reinforced for Arthur first by the Kildare Knot, and later by the Friendly Brothers, and can be found threaded through his life.

He took his duties seriously. He acted as church warden at St Catherine's, the church on Thomas Street, and, along with the rector James Whitelaw and Liberties clothier and fellow warden Charles Haskins, co-signed a report in 1793 on the situation of the manufacturing poor of the parish, focusing on the unemployed, the destitute families of those who had left for the army or navy, and the sick. It described the residents of the parish as being principally 'the working poor, and the wealthy inhabitants are but few', and entreated contributions of aid. He volunteered, and occasionally chaired, the Committee for the Relief of the Poor Unemployed Manufacturers, which by August 1797 had raised over £8,500. Another member of that committee was the MP Henry Grattan, who was also a leading light in the campaign for parliamentary reform and legislative independence for Ireland. Arthur gave 25 years to the Meath Hospital as governor and treasurer, and when the school at St Patrick's needed repairs he was prepared to put his hand into his own purse. In these and many other practical ways he modelled living well and active citizenship.

Although Arthur's origins might be considered humble, he was in fact the child of privilege. It was not the kind of privilege that shielded the landed gentry and many members of the aristocracy from much of the struggle and pain of life, but it was privilege nonetheless. He came from a comfortable home, with a father in steady employment, and a supportive extended family. He benefited from a kind of apprenticeship at his father's side, so that he was quickly able to earn his own living, and to make money not simply from a regular salary but from property investments and the fruits of his own business, first in Leixlip and later in Dublin. He had access to brewing know-how from his maternal grandfather and much later from his stepmother's pub.

His religion actively affected the way he lived his life, but through Protestantism he also benefited from certain structural privileges. Catholics had always been a majority across Ireland, and although Dublin had for a time a majority of Protestants, this was no longer the case by the time Arthur moved to St James's Gate. Sectarian tensions remained. Although, as Arthur's circumstances illustrate, there were plenty of Protestants who did not sit with the élite, almost no Catholics did. The Penal Laws of the late seventeenth century had been designed to restrict Irish Catholics in as many ways as possible. Public office holders had to take the Oath of Supremacy, which placed the British monarch (who could not be a Catholic) ahead of the pope in spiritual and other matters. Education was forbidden for Catholic children, and shortly after Arthur's birth the Disenfranchising Act of 1728 prohibited Catholics from voting.

The Penal Laws were summed up by Edmund Burke, Arthur's almost exact contemporary, as being 'as well fitted for the oppression, impoverishment and degradation of a people … as ever proceeded from the perverted ingenuity of man'. The interdictions were everywhere. Until 1778, at the very time when Arthur was busy getting his new porter ready for market, Catholics and Protestants could not intermarry, nor could Catholics buy land on a lease longer than 31 years. They couldn't even own a horse valued at more than £5. This crushing system had embedded the Protestant Ascendancy as the ruling class and it was only in the late eighteenth century that the chokehold on Catholics began to be released.

As a Protestant, therefore, though neither born into the landowning classes nor part of the Anglo-Irish Ascendancy, Arthur walked the city enjoying freedoms and exercising rights which his Catholic peers could not. Catholic Emancipation was not secured until 1829, well after Arthur's death, but the question of religious equality was tangled up with other significant political events that unfolded in the last few years of his life. Through this lens it is possible to get an insight into how his views translated to politics.

In 1793 the Common Council took a vote on according the freedom of the city of Dublin to Valentine O'Connor. He was a very successful Catholic merchant living in Dominick Street, and active in the Catholic Convention, a representative group of Catholic political leaders which convened in 1792 in Tailors' Hall in Back Lane, the same venue at which the Guild of Brewers and Maltsters had met for a time. O'Connor's wife Mary was one of the daughters of Edward Moore, who advertised in 1784 that his brewery at Mount Brown had 'gone extensively into the brewing of porter'. Arthur must have had at least peripheral knowledge of the family, as O'Connor's father-in-law was effectively both colleague and competition. A report was circulated around town suggesting that Arthur Guinness had voted against O'Connor's admission to the freedom of the city, the implication being that it was through anti-Catholic sentiment. A comprehensive rebuttal of this suggestion appeared in *Saunders's News-Letter* late in 1793:

> We are authorised to contradict, in the most unequivocal terms, a report ... in which it is asserted that Mr Arthur Guinness voted against [Valentine O'Connor]; when the fact is, that Mr Guinness not only voted for his admission himself, but actually solicited several of his friends to vote for him also; indeed, it were absurd to suppose otherwise, from a general view of Mr Guinness's conduct through life, having on all occasions shewn the most anxious desire to have every civil and constitutional privilege which he enjoyed extended to his Catholic brethren; having ever esteemed it the best means of healing divisions, and establishing confidence and affection between his fellow-citizens of every persuasion.

This was a wholehearted public declaration, 'authorised', but in fact probably written, by Arthur, that he wanted to see religious equality, and that he included in this ideal those of 'every persuasion', not simply Catholic and Protestant. This aligned with the views of Henry Grattan, whom Arthur had previously supported. The rebuttal of the suggestion that he voted against O'Connor is couched solely in terms of his desire for equality. There is no mention of his support for O'Connor being based on character. It is perhaps worth noting in this context that Valentine O'Connor, a merchant dealing in wool, cotton, rum, sugar, wine and spirits, owned two-thirds of a sugar estate called Mount William, on St Vincent, including 'its slaves, buildings, etc.'. Given what we know of Arthur's attitudes and beliefs he can only have been opposed to enslavement.

Arthur's tendency was to peaceful progressive patriotism, and he must have believed that Grattan and the other liberal patriots in parliament could deliver, but in 1797, fed up and frustrated, they resigned from parliament. Others were losing patience too, having seen the dramatic result of the French Revolution in 1789, which had galvanised a group of republican Protestants to form the Society of United Irishmen. Theobald Wolfe Tone was a Trinity-educated barrister, Thomas Russell an ex-military man with an Ascendancy background, and James Napper Tandy, in perhaps the closest approximation of Arthur's situation, was a well-to-do merchant and member of Dublin Corporation.

The aim of the United Irishmen was to bring those of all faiths together in the national cause. As Wolfe Tone phrased it:

> [t]o unite Protestant, Catholic and Dissenter under the common name of Irishmen in order to break the connection with England, the never failing source of all our political evils, that was my aim.

When Britain engaged in the French Revolutionary War in 1793, deep suspicion of the United Irishmen could no longer be kept on the back burner. The organisation was outlawed and many senior members went into exile. Wolfe Tone went to America and

then France, where he negotiated with the French to send support
for an armed insurrection. But the dream faltered. In 1796
an attempted French landing at Bantry in West Cork failed in
dreadful weather conditions. The bloody preamble to the actual
rebellion in 1798 was a mess of double-crossing, accusations and
violence. Lord Edward Fitzgerald, commander-in-chief of the
'United Army', and someone Arthur knew through the Kildare
Knot, was arrested about two hundred metres away from the
Guinness brewery. In the scuffle he took a gunshot wound to the
shoulder and, after it became infected, died in Dublin's Newgate
Prison. He was buried in St Werburgh's, in a vault reserved for the
rectors, one of whom was Arthur's eldest son Hosea Guinness.

The rebellion itself was a fragmented and confused affair,
with fighting taking place over the summer, mainly in east
Ulster and Wexford. In Dublin, Arthur's sons Edward and
William Lunell sided with the authorities and joined the Dublin
Yeomanry, a mixed force of Catholic and Protestant loyalist
volunteers, while their brother Arthur II had to stay put at the
brewery. The British response was perhaps predictably brutal. By
the time the French returned under General Humbert in August,
via Killala Bay in county Mayo, things were all but done and
dusted. 'Ireland will be free,' wrote Humbert optimistically to
the Executive Directory of France, seeking reinforcements, but
he surrendered shortly afterwards.

The rebellion had failed, and churning in its wake were
bitter enmities and religious friction. Arthur himself had been
included in a list of 'detestable Traitors, as Spies and Perjured
Informers' published in the *Union Star*: 'Guinness – a brewer at
James's gate, an active spy. United Irishmen will be cautious of
dealing with any publican who sells his drink.' It is hard to know
at this remove whether that kind of accusation stung, angered or
frustrated Arthur. By now he was 73, and must have been begin-
ning to run low on energy, though a 1798 letter from one of his
sons describes him as still going in to St James's Gate every day,

where he stayed 'for an hour or two and sometimes rides out to the Mills; this gives him good exercise which is quite necessary'.

Business was booming, with brewery sales up to 12,000 barrels per annum and £6,000 of profit – £4,000 had already been invested in rebuilding the brewery, and more than £2,000 was still to go into it. The following year would see the last brew of ale: when the rebuild was complete, only porter, of various kinds, would be made. The flour mills were also turning a profit of £2,000. Arthur could see the completion of his work, and knew that, once he was gone, it would be in the safe hands of three able heirs.

But the last years of Arthur's life were not quiet ones. There was more political change to come. After a campaign of vote-buying and bribery with honours, the Act of Union was passed, coming into effect in January 1801. It pulled Ireland into the new United Kingdom of Great Britain and Ireland and catapulted Catholics into the minority. The Irish Parliament was abolished, and Ireland would now have to send MPs to Westminster rather than Dublin. By the end of the 1790s Dublin had hit its stride as one of the foremost European capitals, full of beautiful neo-classical buildings and disposable income. Busy urban lives were catered to in the new courts complex and stock exchange, and these continued to hum with people, while the great parliament building at the heart of the city entered the new century about to be emptied of its MPs and administrative staff, and Dublin steeled herself for the economic and social as well as the political consequences of the union.

For Guinness, a new era was coming too, as the firm sought export markets, and it did so under new leadership. In 1803 Arthur, the 'rugged founder', died at the age of 78, leaving his second, fourth and fifth sons Arthur II, Benjamin and William Lunell to run the brewery. He was buried at his beloved Oughterard.

Arthur Guinness II as a young man.

FOUR

ONE OF MY SONS

The brewery had never operated without its founder at the wheel. Arthur II was now 35, though, and experienced, having worked in the brewery since leaving Whyte's Academy. He had served a kind of apprenticeship by watching, learning from and working alongside his father, and building relationships with key members of the business, before the gradual, managed handover began.

It was a well-planned succession. Bypassing Hosea, the eldest, was no issue. He had already chosen the church, and he had been bequeathed a wonderful inheritance in the form of Beaumont (which he would sell to Arthur II) and properties in Leixlip. Martelli described Arthur II as 'in some ways the most remarkable of all the Guinnesses', and his father, fully understanding his second son's high level of capability, had settled the deeds of the brewery on him when he got married in 1793. 'One of my sons is grown up to be able to assist me in this Business,' he had written in 1790, so when Arthur II had married Anne Lee the property transfer was agreed.

That the leadership of the firm, as well as the property it occupied, was to pass to Arthur II was later made clear by the terms of Arthur's will, which referred particularly to a silver salver which had been presented to him by the Corporation of Brewers of the City of Dublin. The symbolism of the salver was made explicit in the wording of the will:

> during his life the Silver salver presented and given to me
> by the Corporation of Brewers of the City of Dublin and
> after his decease the same to go to the eldest Male branch

of my family then living who shall be in the Brewery
Trade my Will being that the same shall be always here-
after used by such elder Branch of my family who shall
be a Brewer.

Although Arthur was the senior partner by age and designation,
his brothers Benjamin and William Lunell shared his responsibilities. Other key personnel who became embedded in the firm as
trusted colleagues included John Purser, whose son John Purser
Junior and grandson John Tertius Purser also made their careers
in the Guinness brewery.

The Guinness brothers' lives were entwined again and again
by blood, by business and by marriage: ten years after Arthur II's
marriage to Anne Lee, Benjamin married her sister, Rebecca Lee.
They lived in Eccles Street, and had only one child, their daughter
Susan Jane. She grew up to marry, in 1826, her cousin, William
Smythe Lee Grattan, one of ten children born of Arthur II and
Anne Lee. Another of their children, Benjamin Lee, would one
day run the brewery.

The Lee sisters were both dead before this happened, as
both died early, Anne in 1817 and Rebecca in 1819, leaving two
Guinness widowers. Benjamin did not remarry; Arthur married
Maria Barker, who became stepmother to his children with Anne,
but they did not have children together. An 1821 publication, the
Historical Guide to Ancient and Modern Dublin, in a description
of St Werburgh's Church, where Hosea was the incumbent, noted
that there were monuments to Mrs Arthur and Mrs Benjamin
Guinness, 'the wives of brothers of that name, brewers in
Dublin; men extremely conspicuous for piety, integrity and many
Christian virtues; but, above all, charity.'

Arthur II was as civic- and socially-minded as his father
but with an extra helping of religious fervour. Arthur's faith
had been more of a muted backdrop to his life, while Arthur
II's was frequently and expressly invoked, his letters sprinkled

with quotations from the Bible, and exhortations to remember one's heavenly calling. There is some sense of a school report in the opening of a letter Arthur II wrote to his son Benjamin Lee, then 18:

> it gives your dear Mother and me sincere pleasure to see that your hand-writing is improving and that your letters and statement were so neatly and carefully done. We are likewise much gratified by the account your Uncle Ben gives us of your attention to business and that you are endeavouring to make yourself useful.

It is positive feedback, if mildly infantilising for a young man who had already been working in the brewery for two years. Arthur II urges Benjamin Lee to be diligent in his worldly callings but to pay attention to 'higher things ... for we have a Heavenly calling in Christ Jesus and to this our supreme diligence is required'. Benjamin Lee must remember Christ's words about seeking first 'the Kingdom of God and His Righteousness', and to do this in 'the holy Scriptures'.

> Oh then, my dear Boy, read the Bible with care, with earnestness, with diligence, let nothing prevent your daily study of this blessed Book, and as the divine truths it contains are only discovered by the eye of faith, and not by unassisted reason pray earnestly to God that he may be pleased in His infinite mercy to unfold the heavenly treasures of Divine Wisdom to your mind.

And so on, as Martelli drily comments on this letter, for another two pages.

Whenever Arthur cropped up in newspaper reports in the first decade or so after his father's death, it tended to be in the context of helping people: donating to St George's Fever Hospital,

St James's Parochial School, St Catherine's Parochial School and St Paul's charity school; making an annual subscription of five guineas to the Old Men's Asylum, as well as a 20-guinea donation to the building of a dining hall in the asylum; as a member of the Committee of the Society for Promoting the Education of the Poor of Ireland; collecting contributions for the Bethesda Female Orphan School, and the Society of Friends of the Jews.

That was just a selection of the causes he supported, but strong themes of social care, health and education emerge, and very often one or more of his brothers appeared alongside him in the donor or subscriber lists. Reading the reports one after another gives the impression that Arthur was a man who processed numerous requests, and rarely said no. The appeals that piled up on his desk at St James's Gate and at home were not all from charitable organisations, either. The Guinness family was by now very large, and there were a number of poorer relations and connections, some of whom were quick enough to tap up Arthur. This was at a time when the brewery was certainly thriving, but it wasn't turning straw into gold.

Arthur's brother Edward had started off in the brewery, but left and established an ironworks, where after about five years he employed several hundred workers and turned over £170,000 annually. The ironworks seemed initially to be very successful, and benefited from what the *Belfast Commercial Chronicle* referred to as 'all the succour of great capital, and almost inexhaustible private resources', but it fell apart in 1811 and Edward ended up bankrupt and living on the Isle of Man, from where he wrote repeatedly to Arthur for support. By 1815 Arthur enabled him to be bought out of his bankruptcy, thanks to the brewery.

Arthur also had financial worries about his two elder sons, William Smythe Lee Grattan and Arthur Lee. William became a clergyman, and married twice, to a cousin each time. With five sons and three daughters to support on a clergyman's income, he found it hard to manage without injections of cash from his father. At one stage Arthur paid off all William's debts, to the tune of £4,700, and expected him to manage better thereafter, but later had to raise his annual income by £200. 'But unhappily,' Arthur confided to his third son Benjamin Lee in 1849, 'he appears not yet to have learned that a man should depend upon his own means in the use of due economy.' William did get his act together, though, possibly prompted by a discussion between Arthur and William's wife Susan Jane, and in 1850 Arthur wrote more cheerfully that he wanted to restore him to favour, and was 'anxious to receive him with his wife and children to the parental roof from which they have been so long excluded'.

In his 1981 book *The Silver Salver*, the historian Frederic Mullally described Arthur II's second son, Arthur Lee, as 'a slim and pretty aesthete with a carefully arranged forelock', who worked at the brewery but was more interested in writing poetry than making beer. He accrued debt, and once he was out of the hole gave up his brewery shares and his partnership. He did not marry, and had no children, but was popular and social, described by the poet (and family connection) George Darley as 'amiable, excellent', his solicitations and invitations to stay 'the kindest, friendliest'.

The idea of a man being described as 'a slim and pretty aesthete', as some kind of code for his being homosexual, feels more in keeping with the 1890s than the 1980s, when Mullally's book was published. By contrast, in Joe Joyce's *The Guinnesses* it is stated directly that Arthur Lee was homosexual. Of course it was not in the least straightforward to be gay at a time when the prevailing religious morality in Ireland held that homosexual love and acts were wrong, and statute law established that sex between men was illegal. The question of whether Arthur Lee was gay would not necessarily come into play at all were it not for a story about a relationship he is supposed to have developed with a young man who worked at the brewery.

Dionysius Boursiquot was a family connection, a nephew (by marriage) of Arthur's sister Elizabeth. As a family favour he was given a post at the brewery, but he didn't last long in it, and he soon turned up in London, flush with money, to start a career in the theatre. He changed his name to Dion Boucicault and became one of the most successful playwrights of the Victorian era. The story has always been that, after an entanglement with Arthur Lee in Dublin, he was given money for a fresh start elsewhere.

By today's mores, what seems far more problematic than the relationship being between two men is that that at the time of their putative relationship Arthur Lee was a 41-year-old partner in the brewery, while Boursiquot was an employee and still, just about, in his teens. In the 1830s, of course, it was the homosexuality rather than the age difference and power imbalance that made the matter scandalous. No one could be proud of this episode, but it is worth looking at it in the round, to the extent that that is possible. One way of doing so is to consider how Arthur and close family members viewed deviation from the straight and narrow moral path, as illustrated by their charity affiliations.

The constant financial needs of Arthur's family, even after they were grown up and married, with their own families and careers, did not deter him from laying out a sizeable portion of his income in charitable works. The writer James Kelly recently made the point that an after-effect of the Union was that vacancies arose for patrons and governors of various charitable organisations. So many of the nobility left Dublin that the recruitment pool for these positions was drained, and members of prosperous merchant families were able to step into the breach.

The monument to Anne Lee Guinness and Rebecca Lee Guinness in St Werburgh's is a reminder of how little generally has been written about the work carried out by the Guinness women during this period. They were, however, active both alongside their husbands and on their own account. Rebecca was involved with the House of Refuge at 54 Lower Baggot

Street, a shelter for homeless and unemployed women founded in 1802 by Theodosia Blachford, a Methodist and proponent of liberal education for women.

Charities like the House of Refuge sought not just to offer shelter, but also to protect girls and young women from the moral and physical dangers of society, as a 'place of temporary retreat and protection for ... innocent and destitute young females'. Blachford had observed that 'the cause which led many to decline from virtue, and exposed them to innumerable evils' was homelessness. It was young women who were vulnerable, at an 'interesting period of life when the world is new and the mind unaware of its seductions'.

The danger of a sexual fall was always hovering in the wings, and the women who oversaw the House of Refuge (it was run by a committee of governesses) wanted to protect individuals and society. Rebecca drove fundraising as the charity grew, something that was acknowledged in the 1831 *New Picture of Dublin, or Stranger's Guide to the Irish Metropolis*, which included the House of Refuge in a section on charitable institutions.

> In the course of time, the usefulness of the institution being universally acknowledged, but the fund, and size of the building then occupied, inadequate to admit the increasing number of applicants for admission, the late Mrs Benjamin Guinness, whose energy in every good cause was as conspicuous as her judgment in selecting proper objects from its exertion, made great and successful efforts to obtain an increase of public support.

Long after Rebecca's death, she was still being publicly acknowledged as the driver behind the enlargement and improvement of the House of Refuge. Members of her family, including her daughter Susan Jane (by then married to her cousin William Smythe Lee Grattan Guinness) and her brother-in-law Arthur, continued to contribute to the support and development of the home in Lower Baggot Street. Susan Jane Guinness did not just give an annual subscription, but also continued her mother's work by serving as one of the governesses. Rebecca was also active in the Lying-in Charity in Bath, which provided midwifery assistance during childbirth, but also medicines and food where necessary.

Arthur's second wife, Maria, was a contributor to the Harcourt Street shelter for women who had been discharged from prison, and her brother-in-law Hosea gave the use of St Werburgh's for the organisation's annual charity sermon. Maria and Arthur each individually supported the Lock Penitentiary, attached to the Bethesda chapel in Dorset Street, and in the 1830s they were both on the committee at the same time. The penitentiary had been established for women discharged from the Lock Hospital, where they would have been treated for sexually transmitted diseases, or, in the strangled phrasing of the time, 'those baneful disorders which result from incontinence'.

In 1817 the penitentiary housed about 40 such women who 'found a Refuge from Wretchedness and Vice'. While lodged there the women did needlework, calendering (a method for finishing textiles) and laundry, but the aim was to find them secure work situations back in society, or to reunite them with their families. The Lock Penitentiary also relied on an annual charity sermon, but, as there was a connection with the Bethesda chapel, Hosea was not asked to give St Werburgh's for the purpose.

Charity sermons were popular fundraisers, and were advertised well in advance so that people could be sure to be there, and to be seen attending. Sometimes the names of those who had confirmed in advance that they would attend were published in the newspapers, to entice others who might be motivated by the sense of being in a joint endeavour with the rich and famous. For those who didn't attend and donate on the day, donation points were widely advertised, and this was another way in which Arthur, with his city office, could help. It became something of an exercise in naming and shaming to publish the lists of donations, usually in descending order of amount given. Those who dwelt on what other people thought would not wish to be conspicuously absent from the list, nor last on it.

A sample of surviving letters from 1849 begin to illustrate how frequently the cries for help came, and how calmly and unhesitatingly Arthur responded to them. Note after note details repeated, private acts of kindness. The letters show that he lent £300 to a relative in New York, contributed to the upkeep of a 'poor orphan' adopted by Edward Willcocks, paid the school fees of Louisa Day, and supported a widow and her children. His agreement to send the money to New York came with a 'gentle rebuke', so he didn't do it blindly, but he did write cheque after cheque after cheque.

The story of the family's later social work in Dublin, particularly in the early twentieth century, has been told before in Ireland, and almost any Dubliner you stop in the street today would be able to identify Guinness contributions to the built environment and the communities of the Liberties. But the family's belief in putting their profits to work for the benefit of others was in evidence all the way back to the first Arthur.

This kind of charitable work is worth looking at for so many reasons. It gives us a lens through which we can see the kinds of work being done by women in the Guinness family, and shows the kind of social work which was important to the family, men and women. Not all the charitable work undertaken was related to female health and welfare, but it is important to remember that the family's preoccupations through the generations did include sexual health, the fallout of sex outside marriage, and rehabilitating into society those women who found themselves marginalised because of sexual or criminal activity. Seeing Maria and Arthur's names listed together on the committee of the Lock Penitentiary is a reminder that these issues must have formed part of an ongoing conversation between husband and wife.

Perhaps their openness to understanding the reality that people's sex lives were not always contained within the tramlines laid out by society and the churches helped them in taking a compassionate approach to Arthur Lee's experiences. Certainly Arthur referred to his son lovingly in a letter as 'our Beloved Arthur Lee', and also as 'the poor fellow', expressing affection and pity. Perhaps he and Maria were not sufficiently open-minded that they could accept a homosexual relationship, and indeed they would have stood out if they had, but love was not withdrawn from Arthur Lee because of what was, in their eyes, a transgression.

The couple's committee work drives home that their charitable work was characterised not only by financial contributions but by contributions of time, expertise and commitment. It is also a reminder of how precarious anyone's life and condition could feel when there was no real public safety net, and access to welfare services was dependent on privately funded charitable organisations. In later years, as will be seen, Guinness developed a reputation as an excellent employer who could be guaranteed to look after the health and welfare of its workers and their families. These early kinds of charitable undertakings, though, had nothing to do with keeping employees well and happy at work.

It is clear that, during the first decade of his tenure, Arthur had his share of worries and anxieties at home. Work was no easier. By 1811 the brewers were getting increasingly exercised by barriers to their trade, in which they counted the 'excessive use of spirituous liquors', the cheapness of these liquors and the illegal distillation of these liquors. The 'nine principal breweries' of Dublin are listed here, with figures showing their decline in porter sales from 1810 to 1811, as presented to a House of Commons Select Committee in 1811. Each barrel contained 40 gallons of porter.

Messrs.	1810 (barrels)	1811 (barrels)
Egan & Co.	25,950	16,089
Trevor & Keogh	27,424	22,193
Mich. Sweetman	27,424	22,193
Guinness & Co.	70,614	55,488
W. & E. Conlan	21,560	15,678
Grange & Co.	27,463	16,658
Conolly & Co.	50,571	41,595
Madder & Co.	16,807	14,135
Sherlock & Sons	15,547	13,224
Total	280,860	214,777

In the same year the *Picture of Dublin for 1811* reported porter as a 'wholesome and excellent beverage' whose consumption was 'daily encreasing', which sits at odds with the brewers' complaints. However, this publication was intended as a guide for visitors to Dublin and probably indulged in some forgivable talking up of the city and its products. The figures are revealing not just because of what they show about the fall-off in sales, over 66,000 barrels, but also because they show Guinness & Co.'s impressive market share among the principal breweries, at over 25 per cent.

By the early nineteenth century Guinness was no longer to be considered simply a Dublin brewery, in competition with other Dublin breweries. Nationally, the rival was the Cork firm of Beamish and Crawford. In 1800 Beamish and Crawford sold more than six times what Guinness did. Between then and 1814 Beamish and Crawford more than doubled their output, while Guinness increased theirs five-fold, but in 1814 Guinness was still brewing less than half of what Beamish and Crawford brewed. The Napoleonic Wars had been good for Guinness, and their end in 1815 heralded a general depression.

But the 1820s saw things pick up as everyone's eyes were trained on the British export market, and it must have been a thrill for Arthur, Benjamin and William to see not just that their product was starting to be asked for by name, as 'Guinness's Porter', but also that 'Guinness & Co's Dublin Porter' was being advertised for 'exclusive sale' in the city of Chester by Whittle and Jones in 1825, and soon in Bath, Oxford and Manchester. Steamers to Bristol and Liverpool replaced sailing ships and cut sea transport times, while the canal and (especially from the 1840s) rail networks could disperse the casks on arrival. By 1840 more Guinness's porter was being drunk in England than in Ireland.

As far back as 1802, even before Arthur's death, the firm was making porter with an eye to the West Indies market, and the brewer's diary for 1801 considered the problem of keeping beer fresh for long-haul travel. The answer turned out to be the addition of more hops, a natural preservative. But exporting beyond England would not really take off until the 1830s.

The Bank of Ireland had been founded by royal charter in 1783, with a monopoly on the Dublin market. In a public stamp of approval for his commercial and financial abilities, Arthur was elected to the board for the first time in 1804, and again in 1808, the year the bank moved into the vacant parliament building at 2 College Green. From 1810 he remained on the board until 1847, and he served as governor from 1820 to 1822. His holding of this office coincided with the visit to Ireland of the recently crowned George IV in August 1821. The king was due to land south of the city centre at the seaside town of Dun Leary, which was renamed Kingstown later that year. (The name reverted to the Irish Dún Laoghaire in 1920.)

A crowd gathered there to see him disembark, but in order to give him a chance to sober up after the voyage across the Irish Sea, the steam packet *Lightning* killed a bit of time going north across Dublin Bay to land at Howth instead. The king's main interest in visiting Ireland was seeing his lover Lady Conyngham, and he hotfooted it to Slane Castle, where she and her husband were waiting for him. But he did spend some time in Dublin, and as part of his official programme in the city he visited the Bank of Ireland, housed in the magnificent building which only 20 years

ONE OF MY SONS

earlier had bristled with MPs and Lords and the work of the Irish parliament. King George knew this, but a man who had come to Ireland to visit his lover while his wife's funeral was being held in London was not one bothered by nuance or sensitivities.

As governor of the bank, Arthur was the one to receive the king, and to escort him on a tour. The other directors accompanied them, dressed in their special blue silk collars for the occasion, and carrying blue silk-covered batons. The *Belfast News-Letter* recounted the tour of the bank step by step, starting with Arthur conducting the king to 'the great cash office', fitted out for the day with a gallery draped in red cloth and filled with elegantly dressed women. The king was amazed and admired not only the splendour of the apartment but also 'the beauty by which it was surrounded', which might well have encompassed those in the gallery. Arthur continued the tour to the transfer office, across the great hall and through corridors, with more scarlet cloth under-foot, to the armoury, and 'rooms where the machinery is erected for working of the notes'.

Royal refreshments were laid out in the Proprietors' Room, which had been the House of Lords, over two tables to serve 130 'illustrious personages to whom invitations had been presented'. The bank staff wore uniforms and a 'welcome button, so liberally presented to them by the Directors', while the servants wore new liveries. It was reported that the king 'condescendingly conversed' with Arthur, a phrase that did not at the time carry the unpleas-ant sneer it would today, but was almost the direct opposite, suggesting that the king courteously and graciously ignored the difference in social standing between monarch and brewer.

The scene illustrates that, despite what appeared to be a rigid class-based hierarchy, social mobility was possible. From the early nineteenth century, references to Arthur and his sons frequently came with the suffix 'Esq.', suggesting that they were regarded as gentlemen, and now Arthur had met and chatted to the king and been his personal guide around the repurposed parliament building as governor of the bank. The first Arthur could not even have counted on being issued a ticket to the refreshment table; the second Arthur hosted it.

To the second Arthur, a man invested in higher things than worldly callings, the presence of the king as head of the Established Church may have mattered more than His Majesty's 'dress blue coat, with scarlet collar and star, Russia duck trousers and boots'; the state chair, covered in crimson silk edged with gold lace, which was carried about from Dublin Castle to the bank and on to the Mansion House that evening; the peerage shouldering one another out of the way at the 2,000-strong levée at Dublin Castle, where the lost property cupboard the following morning burst with 'shoes, buckles, stars & sword-hilts'; or the 'brilliant fancy dresses and towering plumes' parading around the new round room with which the Mansion House had just been extended.

But even though he was not blinded by glitzy materiality, Arthur cannot have been immune to the sense that he and his family were now operating at a new and more elevated level. His civic, and indeed national, participation was not limited to driving more and more success for the brewery while supporting charitable works and organisations, but also encompassed corporate governance of hefty financial institutions. A supporter of the Union to boot, he was a safe, respectable and genteel pair of hands into which the administration could with confidence pass the king.

Arthur did not shrink from expressing his beliefs. In Mullally's opening to *The Silver Salver*, he wrote that

> [t]he luxury of being able to speak one's mind bluntly and publicly, in defiance of personal consequences, is a prerogative of the dispossessed and of the immensely powerful.

Arthur was neither. He had a good income and a good business, but these were mutable, vulnerable to political upheaval and economic swings and roundabouts. He owned commercial and residential property, but so did many people. He had plenty to lose, materially, and was privileged in many ways, but was not powerful enough to ignore the personal consequences of speaking out. But he spoke his mind 'bluntly and publicly' anyway, unafraid to say what he believed to be right. So far as non-brewery matters went, this characteristic was in evidence both in relation to the king's visit and to Catholic Emancipation.

Twenty-three years earlier, the British administration had quelled the 1798 rebellion, with crown forces carrying out half-hangings, pitch-cappings, floggings and summary executions in the field. The subsequent abolition of the Irish Parliament was seen as the national punishment. By 1821 Ireland was still grieving her dead and transported, and nationalist feeling had not abated. The visit of the king stirred up the anger and grief of many, although there were also those, like Arthur, who believed in the future of the Union. While for the most part the royal visitor was whisked past any evidence that not all Ireland was loyal to him, nor thrilled to see him on Irish soil, there were inevitably a few tricky moments.

One of these, serious enough to be reported in London, was caused by Arthur's own brother-in-law, Frederick Darley, an Orangeman and police magistrate who had married Arthur's sister Elizabeth Guinness in 1785. At the banquet for the king in the Mansion House, Darley called out a toast to 'the glorious, pious, and immortal memory', a reference to William of Orange's victory over his father-in-law James II at the Battle of the Boyne. This toast, guaranteed to inflame Catholic guests, caused a ripple of anger both at the time 'in consequence of which he was, with considerable rudeness, put out of the room', and over the following days, until he apologised.

Daniel O'Connell, despite his total opposition to the Union, felt that a courteous display of loyalty to the king, and evidence of a commitment to a peaceful, religiously integrated Ireland was more likely to serve his nationalist aims in the long run. As the king was about to embark on the journey home from Dun Leary, farewells were offered by a deputation headed by the Lord Mayor and which included both Daniel O'Connell and Arthur. O'Connell knelt before the king and presented him with a crown of laurels. His approach infuriated many of his contemporaries. Byron couldn't get over how enthusiastically the king had been received, and, having digested every report the *Morning Chronicle* printed, he promptly wrote *The Irish Avatar*, a poem which laid into the Irish. The lyricist Thomas Moore, to whom in Paris Byron sent it, approved wholeheartedly, considering it 'richly deserved by my servile & hollow-hearted countrymen'.

Soon printed copies were circulating. O'Connell and Arthur had together attended a meeting to discuss a testimonial to the king, and O'Connell had suggested building him a palace, funded only partly by contributions from the rich, because 'every peasant could from his cottage contribute his humble mite'. This proposal was extraordinary in its financial ambition, its divorce from the reality of peasant life, and its symbolism. Byron didn't miss a trick.

> Aye! "Build him a dwelling!" let each give his mite!
> Till, like Babel, the new royal dome hath arisen!
> Let thy beggars and helots their pittance unite —
> And a palace bestow for a poorhouse and prison!

Arthur's response at the meeting was less rhythmic than Byron's, but then it was given without the benefit of composition time:

> Mr Guinness gave great credit to the Learned Gentleman
> for the overflowing generosity and loyalty of his soul: but
> he thought his suggestion would come better hereafter,
> when they would see how the subscriptions got on.

Arthur may have been a Unionist, but he was also a practical realist, and brought O'Connell down to earth gently. No palace was built. A monument was erected, described by Thackeray as 'a hideous obelisk, stuck on four fat balls, and surmounted by a crown on a cushion', in what was now Kingstown. The monument has suffered over the years from being tarred, and bombed, and graffitied, but remains standing.

Statue to Father Mathew, Cork, photographed in 1877.

FIVE

PROTEST AND PLEDGE

After the king's visit, another eight years passed before Catholic Emancipation became a reality. It was a topic on which Arthur had no hesitation in being vocal, despite knowing that many would disagree with him. His call for equality in a speech made at a meeting of Protestant householders in 1819 came threaded through with loyalist phrasing.

> Our Roman Catholic countrymen and neighbours have expended with us their blood and treasures, in bringing to a happy and glorious termination a war of unequalled length and devastation, and with us should enjoy the undiminished blessings arising from the honourable peace they so eminently contributed to obtain. And I feel a conviction that when they are admitted to a participation of those blessings which the British Constitution is so well fitted to bestow, they will be found as zealous, as steady and as dignified supporters of that Constitution as any sect or class of subjects in His Majesty's dominions.

A petition was left for signatures at the Royal Exchange and the Commercial Buildings, and then Arthur and two others presented it to the Marquis of Downshire, with the request to lay it before the House of Lords, and Henry Grattan with the same request for the House of Commons. Daniel O'Connell addressed a meeting of Catholics in Mary's Lane a couple of months later, and pointed to 'the phalanx of liberal Protestants who came forward on our behalf – the names of the Guinnesses, the LaTouches, the Humphreys'.

Arthur's delight when the Catholic Relief Bill was passed into law in 1829 was genuine. It was a 'joyous moment', as he expressed it at a meeting of the Friends of Civil and Religious Liberty. The Catholic Question should have been more properly known as the Irish Question, he felt, because however sincerely he advocated for Catholic freedoms, he could never look his Catholic neighbour confidently in the face. 'I felt that I was placed in an unjust unnatural elevation above him; and I considered how I would have felt if placed in a different position myself.' Now that what he had so devoutly wished for had come to pass, he was 'much joyed ... My Catholic brother is a freeman. We shall henceforth meet as equals.'

In the wake of the new legislation, O'Connell was able to take a seat as an MP at Westminster, something he had not previously been able to do despite his election in 1828. For several years in the 1820s, O'Connell and Arthur had found themselves more or less aligned, though they were never in lockstep. This didn't survive past the achievement of Catholic Emancipation and O'Connell's concentration on lobbying and agitation for repeal of the Act of Union, which occupied him until his death in 1847.

Despite Arthur's real and articulated support for the Catholic cause, it was repeatedly assumed that, as a Protestant businessman and a Unionist, he did not support it. Perhaps this was not surprising when it was his own family member, Frederick Darley, who had so openly shouted out what he knew to be objectionable to the Catholics present at the Mansion House dinner for the king, in circumstances where a conciliatory atmosphere was the aim. The family's porter was marked out as Protestant and therefore undesirable.

That the religion of the manufacturer could mark the product was made evident in a long satirical sketch published in early 1829. It featured Dublin's three weekly newspapers – the *Freeman's Journal*, the *Dublin Weekly Register* and the *Warder*, meeting in a tavern and discussing what porter to order. 'What is it to us what porter we drink, so it be good?' asks the *Warder*. 'Waiter! Bring us some Protestant porter,' orders the *Register*. 'I'll not be a Dissenter,' says the *Freeman*, at which point the *Warder* calls for some 'Catholic porter too. I only hope that the admixture will produce no internal commotion.'

The perceived embodiment of faiths in particular products is something that persists in Ireland to this day. Associations linger, if more faintly every year: there is Catholic tea and Protestant tea, Catholic whiskey and Protestant whiskey. For Arthur, such satire was probably no more than tiresome, but as Catholic Emancipation was achieved, and through the 1830s the national divide was more clearly drawn on pro- and anti-Union lines, things worsened. When physical attacks were carried out on the brewery and customers, it was much more than tiresome. O'Connell did not advocate violence, and he criticised those responsible, but the attacks continued, and however much Arthur believed in speaking out, having people endangered for delivering, selling or drinking his porter was a brutal consequence.

No carman dared to carry Guinness porter throughout the country, the *Globe* reported in August 1837, so great was the popular indignation against the firm 'for having voted in the late election for the Orange candidates'. According to the newspaper, a man called Thomas Kilduff had come up to Dublin from Roscommon to buy porter from Guinness's, something he had been doing for 35 years. He stayed, as he usually did, at Mrs Butler's, in Bridgefoot Street, and while he was there Mrs Butler and her yardmen cautioned him against buying Guinness's porter. He wouldn't be safe bringing it back to Roscommon, they thought. A representative from Sweetman's brewery called on him and suggested he buy from their brewery instead, even offering to give him a lift up to see the brewery.

Kilduff said he would walk up, but after drinking a sample pint he just wanted to get away, so he fobbed off Mr Sweetman by saying he would come back, and went up to Guinness's as planned. He bought five barrels, packed them onto his dray and set off for Roscommon. Somewhere near the tiny hamlet of Cursis Stream, on the Lucan road, Kilduff's dray was overtaken by a covered car, which then blocked the road. Six men got out and pulled him off his cart, 'saying that he knew well he had no right to bring Guinness's porter to the country'. Someone held him down with a boot on the neck while the others smashed the casks with sledgehammers and crowbars, set the horse off, overturned the dray and did their best to break its shafts.

Nor did violence occur only in out-of-the-way areas. Towards the end of August, the *Pilot*, a newspaper supportive of O'Connell, covered an incident in Dublin's city centre. Four men who went into Hogan's public house in Sackville Place saw that a poster announcing the sale of Guinness's XX ('Double X') had been 'nearly obliterated'. They ordered two glasses of it, but noticed that the proprietor served them porter from another brewery instead. When they queried it, he said he wouldn't sell Guinness's porter for £50. One thing led to another and, amid broken glass and recriminations, the publican rushed round from behind the counter to strike one of the men in the head, saying 'he was the Orangeman he wanted, and he would settle him'.

The following month, wooden casks of porter, waiting overnight on the quay at Broadstone, as was usual before an early-morning transport by barge along the canal, were smashed to pieces and the porter drained into the canal. The police investigation was reported in detail by several newspapers, including the *Freeman's Journal*. Robert Duffy, boatman, who witnessed the attack, described seeing three men who were

> well dressed, wore cloth coats, and seemed to be towns-
> men. They broke the casks with sledges ... and rolled
> the broken casks into the canal; they said nothing during
> the time, but when he asked them why they acted so, the
> three men who guarded the boat where he was said they

would treat him worse than the porter if he said any more about it.

Another witness, James Kelly, in a boat alongside, knew the drays and the men who brought the porter in, so even though the casks were covered with tarpaulin, he 'knew it was Guinness's porter'. He kept safely out of sight, crouched in the cabin of his own boat, while the attack progressed. When challenged about why he didn't get out and raise the alarm, he replied: 'You know that yourself very well. I might get a blow of a stone in the head.' It seemed to be common knowledge that such attacks might take place, and Duffy acknowledged that he had known there was some risk involved in taking the porter, and he refused to do so without indemnity. There was not enough evidence to bring a prosecution against any individual, and so the matter was dropped.

Arthur did not acknowledge, in public at least, that the Kilduff attack stemmed from anything other than commercial rivalries. This seemed to be supported by the timely approach by Sweetman's, who insisted that their approach was ordinary touting for custom, and there was no 'combination of the trade' against Guinness's, and 'that if anything, it was solely among the people, and from political views'. Others were more explicit, and on 16 August Arthur addressed their concerns head on in a letter to the *Pilot*. He wrote, after 'the heat inseparable from a contested election' had subsided, to record what he would have said at the hustings had he been given the chance.

This was that he did not identify with any party, that he disapproved of 'the Orange system, recollecting the evils connected with it', had taken no part in the election except to cast his vote, and had 'never in any way, pecuniary or otherwise, interfered in the matter', nor did he mean to do so. His desire was to see 'honest men on both sides uniting for the maintenance of the constitution while promoting a sound and wholesome reform of its remaining abuses'.

Ten days later an anonymous letter-writer persisted in seeking clarification as to whether or not Arthur had subscribed £1,000 to the election petition against O'Connell, and forced his employees to vote as they were told. If true, this would, the correspondent said, 'justify us all in the resentment felt to the firm of Guinness'. The newspaper wrote that it was not true; Arthur had not given a shilling, nor had he caused anyone who worked for him to vote contrary to their own wishes. Many of them had voted for O'Connell. It concluded: 'We cheerfully do this act of justice to a house on whom so many subsist, both through charity and employment.'

While it would have been satisfying to feel vindicated, Arthur, for whom integrity was so important, must have felt jaded at the repetition of accusations, the atmosphere of bad feeling, the back-and-forth in print. He was nearly 70 by now, but he still had plenty to contend with in his personal and business life, and in the life of the nation. In his later years he also witnessed the temperance movement that opposed his entire business, while, at a remove, he saw his country ravaged by the appalling effects of what became known as the Great Famine.

Arthur had lost his mother in 1817. His brother and business partner, his children's Uncle Ben, died prematurely at 48 in 1826, having been ill for some time. The *Dublin Evening Mail* remembered Ben as 'modest and unobtrusive', a man who seldom appeared in public life. He was a shyer and more private man than Arthur, although, like his brother, he was engaged in a good many charitable works and the management of several charitable institutions. It is obvious that Benjamin was a capable businessman, particularly active in the development of English exports.

His reticence and modesty seem like attractive characteristics, and his good works all the better because he didn't call attention to them, but he remains, like his mother Olivia, an enigmatic character. In the 1830s Arthur and Ben's brother

William Lunell was still active in the brewery, as was Arthur's son Benjamin Lee, whose improved handwriting had so gratified Arthur. Benjamin Lee had entered the brewery in 1814, aged 16, and had become a full partner in 1820. He was to give invaluable support to Arthur through the still difficult years to come, and well before his father's death he would prove his merit as the next leader of the family firm.

Finding an export market in England had been a natural next step for the Guinness brewery, and the uncertain and unsettling atmosphere that persisted in Ireland may have made sales in England even more attractive. Things were going well on that front, summarised by David Dickson as being bolstered by 'full free trade combined with the efficiencies of steam navigation'. In February 1839 Guinness agents Waring and Moline advertised in the *Sun* that they were sole consignees of 'Guinness's Stout for the Metropolis and Eastern Counties', and had agents in London who bottled stout 'with bottle labels bearing the autograph signature of Messrs. Arthur Guinness, Sons, and Co.'.

They were looking for more agents, to cover York, Colchester, Rochester, Chatham, Canterbury, Guildford and Peterborough: everyone wanted Guinness. The bottlers' advertisement for 'Guinness's Stout' is an early printed instance of the change to stout, for which the Guinness brewery would become known worldwide. The official name change followed a period of experimenting with making a 'stouter', or stronger, porter. From 1840 what had been Extra Superior Porter in the brewing logs became Double Stout, and by the time the brewery introduced a trademark label in 1862, it had been renamed again to Extra Stout.

In Ireland, on top of the tense political atmosphere and people being urged not to buy Guinness, the last thing the brewers wanted to hear about was the temperance movement. This was a multi-denominational campaign led by a Catholic friar. Father Theobald Mathew founded the Total Abstinence Society, which encouraged members to pledge their abstinence from all alcohol.

He preached temperance at home (in Cork) and abroad, travelling on a kind of speaking circuit. In Dublin of the late 1830s and 1840s the emphasis of the temperance movement was very much on whiskey and its variations, and the newspaper reported that 'Mathewizing' was already noticeable. Spirit sales began to suffer under heavier duties and lesser demand.

But sobriety was sobriety. It rejected all alcoholic drink, and fourteen thousand people were given temperance medals by the summer of 1839. By the mid-1840s membership numbers were approaching three million. Astonishing as this growth seems, Father Mathew himself asserted the numbers were even higher, over five million by 1842. Elizabeth Malcolm, whose *Ireland Sober, Ireland Free* examines the temperance movement in close detail, suggests that membership numbers did not equate in reality to numbers of people actually pledging sobriety and receiving medals.

Father Mathew based his estimate on the over five million membership cards he sent out in bulk to parishes and temperance centres. Frequently, unused cards were not returned, and sample cards surviving in the National Library of Ireland (including one numbered 5,222,611) are dated and signed by Father Mathew, but have not been filled out with a member's name. These empty membership cards, stacked in parish halls around the country, allowed Father Mathew to envisage what Malcolm calls his 'phantom army'.

Even allowing for a couple of million phantoms, Father Mathew's recruitment was enormous. He had the knack of persuading people to his view that drunkenness was the main culprit when it came to crime, poverty and other social problems. Somewhat surprisingly, he did not have the full backing of the Catholic Church in Ireland in requiring people to pledge total abstinence, for various practical and doctrinal reasons. The church itself did not place an obligation of total abstinence on Catholics, nor did it consider it necessary for anyone else to do so. Naturally enough, some individual Irish priests followed and promoted the temperance cause, and others rejected it. This allowed for the emergence of a brand of temperance which enjoined moderation in drink rather than abstaining from it fully.

There is a story that, during the boycott already described, Arthur entertained an Indian Army officer to dinner, and introduced him to the delights of a Guinness porter. The story may already have grown legs through repeated retellings, but in the version committed to print by Charles Graves in *Ireland Revisited*, the glass of Guinness went down a treat, and the officer remarked that other military men in India would love it too. It would be 'the very tipple', what with wine too expensive, spirits too dangerous and beer too easy to drink too much of.

> "I suppose the demand for it is much greater than the supply?"
>
> "On the contrary," replied Guinness, "Dan O'Connell with his boycott and Father Mathew with his Pledge have half ruined me between them."
>
> "Is that so?" said the Army Officer ruminatively. "Now look here, Mr Guinness, suppose I take a consignment of this good stuff out to India and introduce it for you there?"
>
> "Well, sir, India is a far cry, but if you really care to make the experiment I shall be only too delighted to back it with a good commission."

So, despite the boycott (a word which did not actually enter usage until 1880) and the Total Abstinence Society, there were new markets to explore, and the Indian experiment worked in the brewery's favour. In any event, the temperance movement in Ireland began to lose momentum from the mid-1840s. Father Mathew shifted his focus from Ireland and brought his campaign to England and Scotland, and, after the Famine, to the United

States, until his death in 1856. The Knights of Father Mathew, an organisation designed for Irish emigrants who wanted to live a temperance life, was founded in St Louis in 1872.

In 1843, O'Connell, as part of his campaign for repeal of the Act of Union, convened a series of 'monster meetings', including one at the Hill of Tara supposed to have been attended by a million people. The meeting planned for Clontarf was hastily cancelled when an army presence showed how serious the government was about squashing such sizeable demonstrations. O'Connell and his son John O'Connell were arrested. O'Connell, reported one newspaper, as 'a bailed and arraigned traverser in the Court of Queen's Bench', was 'indeed much less potent than as a *quasi* king of Ireland, traversing the land from Tara to Mullaghmast'.

While the movements led by Father Mathew and Daniel O'Connell looked as if they might be running into the sand, at St James's Gate Arthur and Benjamin Lee kept their commercial heads engaged. They believed that Ireland could and should flourish within the Union, and that wanting what they saw as the best outcome for Ireland was a patriotic position. Economically, there was no doubting that the Union had been good for the firm, enabling the freer movement of Guinness to England, and by now the brewery had consolidated sufficiently to be ready to expand its export markets. If India called, St James's Gate would answer.

Within Ireland itself, there was ground to be made up. In 1836 there were 19 ale and porter breweries in Dublin, and though this number dropped to 11 in 1880, the total output was far greater. Through the 1840s it was porter rather than whiskey or ale that people wanted in rural Ireland, and by 1864 the Guinness brewery was supplying more than half of the beer sold in Ireland.

By far the most significant event of the mid-nineteenth century in Ireland was the Famine. Ireland of course experienced not a famine but rather a protracted period of starvation, poverty and disease in the wake of the failure of a single crop, potatoes, the main food source for millions in rural Ireland. This distinction is made in the Irish name, an Gorta Mór, which translates as the Great Hunger, but even this somewhat more accurate name cannot render the full horror of the period. It brought grief and suffering of such relentless intensity that it marks the psyche of the Irish people today. This is the subject of scholarly research across a number of areas including mental health and gene expression.

Babies gestated during the Famine accounted for the increase in asylum admissions on mental health grounds as they reached maturity from 1860 to 1870. Epigenetic effects of trauma are lasting biological changes first in the children, and later in subsequent generations, of survivors. Even those who simply witnessed it were traumatised. Violet Martin, one of the authors of the late nineteenth- and early twentieth-century *Irish RM* books, described her parents' early experience of 'the starving tenants … impossible to feed, impossible to see unfed' in Galway, and of the Famine's long reach: 'the Famine yielded like the ice of the Northern Seas; it ran like melted snows in the veins of Ireland for many years afterwards'.

Martin also remembered that '[t]he rapid pens of my father and mother sent the story far', and that help came, for example, from English Quakers who 'loaded a ship with provisions and sent them to Galway Bay'. At the same time, many people in comfortable urban settings were not fully aware of the extent of the damage battering the country, or were aware, but found it more comfortable to shutter themselves. While it took months for a full realisation to dawn in Ireland itself, it appears to have taken years for the full impact to have been appreciated in England.

The Guinness family archive contains a letter to Arthur, written in January 1847 by the Rev. William Paul Dawson. He was the Protestant rector of Kilmore Erris, just about as far west as it is possible to get in Mayo, a county then in the grip of devastation. He said it was impossible to describe the agony of those, both Catholic and Protestant, living in his parish, 'far far beyond my words to express'. It was getting worse every day, and 'frightful beyond all description to see the sufferings of these poor creatures & wonderful to behold their patience'. Although the two men did not know one another, Dawson had heard of Arthur's 'great benevolence and charity', and asked for assistance, although by this point money was not necessarily the answer.

> The Govr^t. Depots are shut and provisions withheld by the Commissary he refused to sell out to me any yesterday tho' I had some money from the Nat Club £15 which w^d. have given to my own poor Parishioners and a number of Roman Catholics immediate relief.

These depots had been established to sell the government-supplied Indian corn, christened 'Peel's brimstone' after the prime minister, and detested, as it was next to impossible for the starving Irish to digest. It was desperately frustrating to know there was food inside while people died outside. As Dawson closed his letter to Arthur, he seemed on the verge of being overwhelmed by what he faced.

> I am distracted with the constant appeals … and it is most affecting to be without the means of relieving their wants while I am writing crowds are about my house begging & imploring for aid that I scarcely know what I am writing.

It would be understandable if he had become overwhelmed. Asenath Nicholson, who wrote a contemporary account of the Famine, referred, on a visit to Belmullet, to the well-known 'sad fate of the Protestant curate', who had entered the asylum. Locally, it is said that this was Dawson, that his intolerable situation drove him to drink, and the asylum. He died in October 1849.

Arthur was alarmed by further reports from the west. He was rather old and ill by 1849, and was staying at Torquay on the Devon coast hoping to experience some health benefits. While there he read a letter from a newspaper correspondent who had just returned from Connemara, the part of Galway that was home to Violet Martin and her parents. Arthur wrote, appalled, to his trusted Benjamin Lee, that the correspondent presented:

> a picture of the state of destitution in Conemara [*sic*] exceeding in horror and misery anything we have before observed. May the Lord in his infinite mercy direct our Government and all individuals also possessing means to do so to the use of measures to relieve if possible the sufferings of our wretched poor people. I wish to know any mode in which we might be able to aid in the work. You know my dear Ben that my purse is open to the call.

Arthur disbursed money to countless charitable causes, family members and friends of friends, and it is clear from what he wrote to Benjamin Lee how affected he was by one description of what was happening, and how keen he was to help. His brother Hosea was a clergyman, and so was their nephew, the Rev. William Newton Guinness, at that time vicar of Ballisodare in Sligo. He and Dawson were both members of the Diocese of Killala and Achonry, both members of the Church Education Society, and in 1845 had been co-signatories to a public letter about the use of the scriptures in the new national education system. So if Arthur had needed to ask around within the family, to contextualise Dawson, he could readily have done so.

Dawson's appeal specifically sought to relieve both Protestants and Catholics, exactly the kind of non-sectarian approach of which Arthur approved, and he also sought it as a minister of the church, which would have appealed to Arthur's piety. Arthur kept Dawson's letter, which suggests that it mattered to him. Although the family archive has not yielded a copy of Arthur's reply, it seems impossible, given what I know of him, that he did not respond as Dawson hoped he would, and as I hope he did.

Arthur had not, however, been able to identify a public scheme through which the brewery could deliver financial aid: he wrote of his disappointment that there was no movement 'independent of sectarian or party spirit' in aid of the relief of the destitution in the west and south. 'If there were I know how ready our firm would be to stand forward.' His language suggests that whatever sting had lodged during the challenges of the 1830s was still painful, leaving him reluctant to be publicly associated with one political or religious affiliation or another.

Arthur II's son Arthur Lee, from his home Stillorgan Park in county Dublin, had clearly been active in relief efforts before 1849, given that already by 1847 he had been presented with a small green marble obelisk, inscribed:

> To Arthur Lee Guinness, Esq., Stillorgan Park. To mark the veneration of his faithful labourers who in a period of dire distress were protected by his generous liberality from the prevailing destitution. This humble testimonial is respectfully dedicated consisting of home materials. Its colour serves to remind that the memory of benefits will ever remain green in Irish hearts.

This marble memento is at Elveden today.

In the immediate aftermath of the Famine the Encumbered Estates Court was set up to offer landowners still struggling underwater an efficient mechanism for getting their affairs in order. The court cleared up the title, ascertained liabilities and sold the estate on with a parliamentary title. The purchase money paid off outstanding claims, with the balance going to the original proprietor. Benjamin Lee Guinness was in a position to buy up land, and there was plenty becoming available in Connemara. He started with Ashford Castle by Lough Corrib in Cong, owned by Lord Oranmore and Browne, in 1852, and followed up with nearby and adjoining estates as they came on the market, so that by 1871 he had 20,000 acres across three baronies in counties Galway and Mayo. It was certainly great personal enrichment occasioned by the effects of the Famine. The bitter taste that this leaves can be very slightly sweetened by the fact that Benjamin Lee embarked immediately on a series of improving works, including draining and reclaiming bog and wasteland, and building roads, which employed a few hundred local people.

The Famine scarred the whole country, including the cities. Between 1847 and 1850, Charles Knight published the eight-volume work *The Land We Live In*. While it foregrounds the beauty of the Irish scenery and urban architecture, the book finds Dublin in a depressed and neglected state. In the 1860 publication *Ireland: Its Scenery, Character &c* by the husband-and-wife travel writers the Halls, Dublin is depicted in high definition as a city down on its luck. The Liberties area, within which St James's Gate sits, was noted for having a thriving textile industry, and the colossal brewery, but little else. The whole area, like many in the city centre, was in a chastened state. '[L]arge houses of costly structure everywhere present themselves ... all attest the opulence of its former inhabitants', but those houses were now crammed with numerous families.

It was a preview of the kind of urban poverty that would come to define Dublin's slums into the early twentieth century, and it had long roots. As well as the million or more people who emigrated during the Famine, there was a huge movement of the rural poor who, without any surviving connection with land or family members, drifted towards urban centres in search of shelter and work. Many of these ended up in the multiply subdivided city-centre houses that had once been homes to single families. Here in the city people could reinvent themselves without speaking of the pain of the past. Irish society in the post-Famine years changed, despite the still-spreading bruises of the Hungry Forties. Some of this was at least partially ascribable to the loss of 20 per cent of the population, stripped away from the very poorest stratum.

Changes in life after the Famine were, predictably, unevenly felt. As was usually the case, the more comfortable you were, the more comfortable you became. But overall, housing stock improved, the marriage age rose and the consumption of luxury goods like tea and tobacco increased. People's daily habits changed too, as the retail economy blossomed. More and more manufacture shifted to urban areas, while cottage industries and home-produced goods fell off. The railways whisked travellers past towns and villages that might otherwise have offered refreshment and a room for the night. Areas of the country were unpeopled and desolate. Farmland was covered with livestock, tillage more or less abandoned. Houses that might once have housed several generations of a family stood empty while their stones dropped back in to the land.

Arthur died in June 1855, at Beaumont. He was 88. Benjamin Lee mentioned in a letter of 13 June that his father had wanted a funeral 'free from all parade', and so, although various connections in commerce, such as the members of the Grocers' and Vintners' Trade Protection and Benevolent Society, were anxious to attend and pay tribute, it was decided to keep it private. As it turned out, there was no keeping people away from the funeral of a man who had earned such respect and affection.

When his remains were taken from Beaumont, and borne to Mount Jerome Cemetery at Harold's Cross, a funeral procession described as being a full two miles long sprang spontaneously into being. The Lord Mayor of Dublin led in his carriage, and great numbers of brewery workers brought up the rear in a selection of cars and carts. Many present had personal as well as commercial relationships with him, like the faithful and capable John Purser, whose family had for so long contributed to the steady success of the brewery.

Other familiar names, some mercantile, some aristocratic, some with a toe in each pool, included Liberties whiskey makers John Jameson and Henry Roe; the Earl of Meath, whose 'Liberty' centred on Thomas Street; James Stewart, now Governor of the Bank of Ireland; and Sir John Kingston James, Dublin wine merchant, twice Lord Mayor of Dublin, created a baronet in 1823. A number of churchmen were also present. John Gregg, soon to be made Bishop of Cork, knew Arthur from his days as chaplain of the Bethesda chapel in the 1830s; Denis Browne, the Dean of Emly, conducted the service. Arthur was buried in the family vault. The Guinnesses were Dubliners now.

St Patrick's Cathedral, Dublin, photographed in 1877.

SIX

BREWER'S BOUNTY

When Arthur II died in 1855, his son Benjamin Lee Guinness was already 57, and very far removed from the 'dear boy' to whom Arthur had once written his loving letters. Benjamin Lee had lived a full adult life and had a profitable and challenging career in the brewery. But he had never yet had to do it without his father at hand to advise and steady him. His solo run would, as it turned out, be short enough, at 13 years, but in the Guinness way, he would pack a lot in.

Benjamin Lee and his brother Arthur Lee had initially lived together at Thornhill in Clontarf, a 50-acre estate that they extended by buying up adjoining lands whenever they became available. Benjamin Lee had married his 27-year-old cousin Elizabeth Guinness in 1837, and at that time he rebuilt Thornhill as a brand-new house that he called St Anne's. He bought his brother out in 1838, coincident with Arthur Lee's leaving the brewery and the partnership. The resulting arrangement seems to have been a happy one all round. Benjamin and his new wife had four children: Anne, known as Annie, in 1839; Arthur Edward, later Lord Ardilaun, in 1840; Benjamin Lee, known as Lee, in 1842; and Edward Cecil, later the Earl of Iveagh, in 1847.

The young family settled in St Anne's, while Arthur Lee settled in Stillorgan House, with its views of the mountains and the sea, where he would stay for the next 20 years. St Anne's was five or six miles from St James's Gate, close enough for comfort, and yet sufficiently far away and self-enclosed to feel like a completely different world. It had a gorgeous view of Dublin Bay from the north side, as did Stillorgan House from the south, and was sheltered by a thick belt of trees from the sights and sounds of the main road that ran along the shore. It offered Benjamin Lee's young family the chance to enjoy life on a country estate while being very close to Dublin city centre.

Benjamin Lee revelled in his family. He wrote to and about them with a freely expressed affection that suggests they always knew how valued they were. He had felt the affection of his own father, and he was open in passing this on. Even after 25 years of marriage, when he and his wife were apart they still wrote letters to one another as sweethearts, their customary opening 'My Own Sweet Love'. Elizabeth, who signed herself Bessie to her husband, would refer to their children as 'the Pets', while he would call them 'the Babes'. In their letters health was a constant concern: their own, the children's and other people's, though their own and the children's were addressed in the most urgent terms.

For example, in 1859 Benjamin Lee ('B.') reports that their eldest, Arthur, has had a headache, has ridden from St Anne's to St James's Gate and back, and walked to church. 'Your poor pet thought himself quite well yesterday morning, but got a little rain when riding to town and feels the throat very very little today – otherwise perfectly well.' This pet was now a fully grown 19-year-old and might have been expected to be able to cope with a slight headache and some drizzle while riding, but the well-known Victorian preoccupation with health was on the rise. This language was echoed years later in love letters from their youngest son Edward to his future wife Adelaide, when he signed himself off 'Ever old pet's fond Neddy'. It is sweet to think of him reaching for the words of affection familiar to him from childhood.

Those people who were more peripheral, but had more serious issues, were dealt with in rather less detail. In 1862 Elizabeth writes to her son Arthur that, in her own diagnosis, she had nearly died: 'The evening before your dear Papa came I was so weak and breathless I thought I might soon be at rest'

– but she pulls through. She is not sleeping well, and her circulation is 'so very rapid, just I think from some struggle in the poor framework', i.e. her body. In the next paragraph, 'Edward enters [Trinity College] on Monday next privately as his Tutor seems to be dying and could not go on with him', something about which she is remarkably matter-of-fact for one so alive to the ever-present possibility of death. In the next, her second son Lee is 'better but not well', while Elizabeth herself has one final issue to mention, which is 'a gastric attack'.

She writes to Benjamin Lee in the same year hoping that he and the Pets, who have just docked at Southampton, have 'no colds after the heat in Paris'. Bessie herself is 'doing well and getting straight especially the bone wonderfull quickly', although she is worried about going away for the winter as she has always felt 'the delicacy of chest and liability to cough' was brought on by travelling. She is sorry to hear that 'poor dear Lee looks poorly' and advises that everyone take care in the change of weather. This advice is especially important for 'my own Sweetest One. What extacy [sic] to think of having him so soon'. A postscript urges Arthur to watch over his younger brother Lee 'and coax him to be wise and not be up late'.

At this remove there is a slightly oppressive sense about all this, as though she were convinced that she and those around her were constantly on the brink of death, and that that possibility was all she could focus on. Having said that, Elizabeth did die at 51, so perhaps she was right to be so anxious about her health and everyone else's. Besides, she and Benjamin Lee were clearly absolutely mad about each other, still experiencing one another's presence in terms of 'extacy', so it may simply have formed part of their love language to interrogate one's welfare to this detailed extent. Their letters were for one another, and not for us.

Things were going well at the brewery, and Benjamin Lee was inspired to buy a new townhouse in Dublin. St Stephen's Green had been levelled and designed as a recreation ground in

1670. It had been carefully enclosed by a low wall set with gates and turnstiles. Gravel walks, lined on either side with trees, were laid out just inside the perimeter. The walk on the north side, the Beau-walk or the Beaux Walk, was the place to go to show off your fashionable clothes, and Lewis's 1787 *Guide to Dublin* compared it to the Mall in St James's Park, 'the scene of elegance and taste'. The inner area was laid out in lawn, with a statue of George II on horseback.

Standing on the south side of the Green, number 80 was a graceful Georgian mansion designed by Richard Cassels in 1730 for the Bishop of Killala. Mary Delany visited it the year after it was built. To her eye, it was

> *magnifique* … the chief front of it is like Devonshire House. The apartments are "handsome", and furnished with gold-coloured damask, virtus, busts, and pictures that the Bishop brought with him from Italy. A universal cheerfulness reigns in the house. They keep a very handsome table, six dishes of meat are constantly at dinner, and six plates at supper.

But, like many large houses in Dublin, number 80 fell vacant after the Act of Union, when the loss of the Irish Parliament resulted in a drain of money and people from the capital. The Green itself also fell into disrepair, with parts of the perimeter wall in pieces, and gardening work neglected. In 1814 the park was made accessible only to residents of the Green, and a group of commissioners took on the responsibility of redesigning and maintaining it. They laid out new walks, and replaced the old perimeter walls with black iron railings around the Green's mile-long circumference. Keys were issued to householders. A wave of resentment rippled through the rest of the citizens, who had for so long been entitled to walk in the garden, and were now faced with locked gates.

In 1809, shortly before this change in status, the Master of the Rolls, John Philpot Curran, had with some prescience bought the neglected number 80, and after several more changes of ownership Benjamin Lee bought it in 1856. This handsome house was where the family would from now on spend their winters. For Benjamin Lee it was a shorter and less mucky drive or ride to work at St James's Gate than it was from St Anne's, and a house on the Green was perfect for city entertainment at scale. A few years later, Benjamin Lee bought the house next door, number 81, and he opened the two houses up into one. Decorative work, the construction of a pond and temple in the garden, and some necessary stabling and coach houses totted up to £12,873.

Behind these two houses, running more or less parallel to the Green, was a pleasure ground known as Coburg Gardens, which had originally been the slightly awkwardly placed front garden of the Earl of Clonmell, who had to cross Harcourt Street to get to it. Benjamin Lee bought these 11 acres in 1862, and would make them available as a site for the Dublin International Exhibition of 1865. All of this St Stephen's Green property, plus the full 22 acres of the Green, would over time be gifted to the Irish people. For now, this was home for Benjamin Lee, Elizabeth and their family. Their youngest boy, Edward Cecil, Ned to the family, was nine. It was the ideal age for park walks in the Green, and as, unlike his older brothers, he was not sent away to school, but educated at home, he was able to make use of it.

London's ambitious Great Exhibition of the Industry of All Nations in 1851 saw 14,000 exhibitors from 34 nations display 100,000 products, in a purpose-built glass building. This huge, technologically innovative Crystal Palace was designed and built on a 19-acre site in Hyde Park, conceived by architect and engineer Sir Joseph Paxton, head of the Duke of Devonshire's gardens at Chatsworth. The exhibition ran through the fine months, May to October. Britain and her empire dominated the displays, determined to show the world that imperial might was matched by industrial power.

While the Great Exhibition was an enormous success when measured by footfall and impact, it wasn't a universally popular project, either at home or in the colonised countries, which were called on to contribute. Its focus on the creation of wealth through industry drew bitter criticism from John Ruskin, for example, who had no time for the capitalist ethos which drove it. He was contemptuous of the lauded Crystal Palace, and rejected the idea that this greenhouse, 'larger than ever greenhouse was built before', had any artistic significance. Mechanical ingenuity and structural enormity, features of 'a screw frigate, or a tubular bridge', were impressive, but did not raise the Crystal Palace into the realm of poetry or painting so far as he was concerned.

The exhibition served many purposes, and pure showing off was certainly one of them. But it was also positioned as a useful entertainment for ordinary people, and after the first three weeks of the exhibition a reduced entry fee of one shilling came into operation (except on Fridays and Saturdays). Four and a half million people paid the shilling entry fee, and a million and a half more paid full price.

Anything so ambitious and extravagant naturally drew a multiplicity of reactions. The Crystal Palace was at once impressive, seductive, overwhelming, distasteful, gorgeous, mighty and devoid of artistic significance. But everyone was talking about it, including people in Ireland, and the first Irish exhibition was held in Cork the following year. In 1853 came Dublin's turn with the Great Industrial Exhibition, in connection with the Royal Dublin Society, held on the lawn of Leinster House in Kildare Street.

One exhibitor at the Dublin exhibition was wood carver Richard Barrington Boyle, who had carved an oak hall chair for St Anne's. Benjamin Lee lent Boyle the chair for the exhibition so that he could show all his best work. The Dublin exhibition was nothing like so huge in scale as London's, and did not aim for international participation, but there was nonetheless some-thing transformative about it for Ireland. The Mayor of Cork, rightly proud that his city had been in the vanguard, said that Cork had 'given a tone to all Ireland, and infused a hopeful spirit into the breast of a country which had every provocation to despair'. There was to be a measure of post-Famine healing in this display of energy, capability, self-reliance and the richness of Irish creations.

It was in this context that the first murmurings began about a new exhibition, to be called the Dublin International Exhibition. Although the concept originated with the Royal Dublin Society, they were not solely responsible for its execution. A company was set up to oversee the design and construction of a suite of buildings for a permanent exhibition, as well as concerts, lectures, tempo-rary gallery exhibitions and a winter garden and conservatory.

The Dublin Exhibition Palace and Winter Garden Company was launched early in 1862, with three trustees: the Duke of Leinster, Lord Talbot de Malahide and Benjamin Lee Guinness. Certainly, Benjamin Lee was in exalted company with the other trustees, if elevation was measured in the ranks of the peerage. It may have been as much of a thrill for him to host, in his elegant St Stephen's Green mansion, meetings chaired by a duke as it had been for his father to entertain the king at the Bank of Ireland. And there was a greater intimacy at home. But there is no doubt, looking at the list of directors, of the value brought to the table by the experience and competence of his commercial peers.

There were 43 directors, most of whose names were attached to Dublin's business successes of the mid-nineteenth century, including John Switzer, of the department store; George Roe, of the distillery; Thomas Gresham, of the Sackville Street hotel; John Fry, of the silk and poplin firm; Alexander James Ferrier of the department store Ferrier & Pollock; Thomas Pim, linen and poplin manufacturer; Maurice Brooks, interiors; William Russell, tea merchant; and Robert Collis, co-founder of McBirney's department store. Other talent came in the form of engineer William Dargan, who had designed and built the railway from Dublin to Kingstown in 1833, and had led the planning and execution of the 1853 exhibition; and the designer of the Crystal Palace, Sir Joseph Paxton, now a Liberal MP. These were men – and they were all men – who had enormous ability, and had put that ability usefully to work.

Benjamin Lee was able to put the Coburg Gardens site at the disposal of the Dublin Exhibition Company, and it was decided to build the exhibition palace there. The development was intended, at this point, to include a winter garden, concert hall, art gallery, science museum and lecture theatre, public bazaar and ornamental pleasure ground, all in the service of 'rational amusement', and run on a commercial basis. Despite Benjamin Lee's provision of the Coburg Gardens, there were those pushing to have the building erected in the centre of St Stephen's Green, and pointing out that this would be the perfect opportunity to bring the Green back into public use. The *Dublin Daily Express*, for example, darkly noted that it didn't think much of a site 'to the rere of stables, with the back windows of the houses looking upon the visitors'. On the other hand, an *Irish Times* letter-writer remembered a foundered attempt to build something similar in the Portobello Gardens, and thought the Coburg Gardens, so convenient to the suburban rail stations, was the perfect spot.

The company issued a prospectus offering 10,000 shares, at £5 per share, and opened a competition for designs for the building. By September 1862 the competition entries were gathered into a public exhibition of proposed designs. Shareholders could pick up complimentary tickets, while members of the public got in for sixpence. The assessing panel found that none of the entries met the building's stated requirements within the stated budget of £35,000, and so, among loud grumbling from other competitors, the contract was awarded to Alfred Gresham Jones, with the stipulation that alterations would have to be made to bring the project to affordability. This would be done with the help of Frederick Darley, advising architect to the Dublin Exhibition Palace and Winter Garden Company.

Darley, a cousin of Benjamin Lee's and son of Frederick Darley Senior, who had behaved so badly with his toast at the banquet for the king in 1821, oversaw the new layout of the 15-acre site. There, Jones's design, a vast iron and glass structure, would be built amid the new pleasure gardens and athletics grounds emerging from what the *Freeman's Journal* described as 'the uneven, trampled, and most anti-picturesque' Coburg Gardens. Benjamin Lee removed his southern garden wall, leaving the lake, centred on its granite temple, as a boundary between his garden and the public space.

The levelled, drained site was mainly in grass, with trees and hedges planted inside the 12-foot-high surrounding walls. The more structural elements of the gardens began to emerge: a three-acre sunken archery ground, a huge rock grotto with cascading water, a maze and a series of avenues and serpentine walks. Soft, luxurious planting schemes included rhododendrons, ferns and mosses, and these, with the evergreens and trees, were embedded ahead of the building work, so that they would have time to mature. During the construction period the building ground was separated by hoardings, and the structure rose up within a scaffolding extraordinarily quickly. The work was carried out by the firm of Beardwood, who put at least 300 men to work on the site, and eight months into the project the central portion was ready for roofing.

Dubliners were excited at the prospect of having access to this new Winter Garden and the surrounding pleasure ground, and it must have given Benjamin Lee a huge amount of pleasure to see the work progressing, even if his duties as a trustee of the company were time-consuming and often wearisome.

Edward Cecil, nine when the family had moved to St Stephen's Green, was now 15. He was old enough not only to be fascinated by what was being created more or less in his back garden, but also to understand its significance, and to play his part in discussing the developments with his father, both at home and on their trips to and from the brewery, where Edward was now at work. A diary entry for 29 October 1861 had recorded: 'Walked home with Papa from James Gate', a half-hour walk offering plenty of time to chat.

A couple of days earlier they had also visited the Royal Dublin Society exhibition in Kildare Street, where Joseph Kirk's plaster version of a marble Sappho he had made for Benjamin Lee was on display. Eleven years later, when Benjamin Lee was dead, and the sculpture had passed to Edward Cecil, he would himself lend Kirk's marble Sappho, along with many other artworks, to Dublin's 1872 exhibition, perhaps remembering being with his father and seeing her *in situ* in Kildare Street. This Sappho is still at Farmleigh today, sitting bathed in light, with her lyre on her knee, in the conservatory.

These times in the company of his father were just as formative for Edward Cecil as his brewery apprenticeship, and they also enabled Benjamin Lee to get to know his youngest child. The walk home from the brewery wound past St Patrick's Cathedral, and this too must have sparked conversations. As is obvious from the letters already quoted, Benjamin Lee's Christian faith was important to him, not just as a background to his life, but informing his thinking and his desires. Church attendance mattered. The cathedral was the Church of Ireland church closest to home at number 80, and to be a member of its congregation and to worship there must have given Benjamin Lee deep peace.

The cathedral has occupied its current site since the thirteenth century, when it was built on what was pretty marshy land by the River Poddle. Its early history is full of the drama of floods, fires, storms, blown-down spires and, in the mid-sixteenth century, the collapse of the great stone roof. The cathedral boasted a grammar school, an almshouse and Dublin's first public clock, erected on the steeple in 1560. By then the cathedral needed attention, and after a public appeal the roof was repaired and buttresses added, but there were more serious underlying issues.

By the end of the eighteenth century the south wall was significantly out of the perpendicular and the roof was propped up by wooden supports, and it was too dangerous to hold a service there. The nave roof needed redoing, as it couldn't sit on wooden props forever, while the stone roof over the choir was so heavy that the piers were eventually going to give way. Parts of the building were exposed to the weather, and by 1845 the western wall of the south transept was, in Dean Pakenham's words, 'rent from the roof to the ground, and is now supported almost entirely by flying buttresses, erected in the sixteenth century, which are themselves by no means safe'. The building was a mess of patch-worked repairs and no repairs at all, and the more time passed without remedy, the more opportunity the rain had to degrade the building's fabric. With the Famine now ruining lives up and down the country, any available funds were being diverted to relief works, and it was not until the 1860s that an opportunity to save the cathedral was presented.

It was Benjamin Lee who presented it. In 1860 he offered, in a letter to the Dean and Chapter, to assist in the necessary repairs, and asked them to entrust to him

> unrestrictedly and without any interference such parts of this sacred & time honored building as may be necessary for the purpose. I will endeavour with God's assistance to restore them (so far as may be practicable) to their former state – No deviation from the original architectural design (however slight) shall be permitted and I will hold myself personally responsible to the Dean & Chapter that those parts of the Cathedral with which I may interfere shall be restored by me to a state of perfect & permanent repair.

The *Freeman's Journal* reported delightedly that this 'big hearted Irishman' wanted the materials and workmanship to be Irish wherever possible, and that he employed 'nothing on this building but Irish labour, knowing well that … Irishmen, if properly encouraged would be second to no men.' Five bays on the nave's south aisle, the wonky walls, a disappeared triforium, the clerestory windows and the nave roof were all remade, along with other more minor structural works. The screens and partitions which had been put up over the years were removed, and the cruciform footprint of the building was revealed to the congregation for the first time in several generations.

Ambitiously, Benjamin Lee chose to supervise the works himself, which meant that when criticism came, it can only have stung. The well-known ecclesiastical architect J.J. McCarthy wrote a scornful letter to the *Dublin Builder*, enumerating what he considered the architectural and stylistic errors of the work. The *Dublin Builder* printed it, while offering a counter view. Someone, perhaps Benjamin Lee, marked up the letter in delicate pencil on the newsprint. This copy of the newspaper has been kept ever since, along with original reports of the condition of the cathedral, with the family papers.

Benjamin Lee also made sure to finish the job with decorative work, a new pulpit and a magnificent stained-glass window at the west end that illustrated 39 episodes in the life of St Patrick. He recast the fifth bell in the tower, and had two new ones made, in F and C#, to be used with the carillon clock. Each of his bells carries the inscription '*Spes mea in deo* B.L.G. 1864', meaning, 'My hope is in God'. On a still, quiet day the ringing of the bells would have reached Benjamin Lee's ears as he stood on the threshold of the brewery or his doorstep in St Stephen's Green.

The years since his father's death had been busy and expensive for Benjamin Lee, with the work on both the cathedral and the exhibition palace, both public buildings, one so ancient and one so modern, one serving Dublin's spiritual needs and one showcasing its material innovations. His personal expenditure had also been high, and not just because of his purchase of the St Stephen's Green houses and the acreage of the Coburg Gardens. He was living well, to put it mildly.

When his only daughter Annie married the Rev. William Conyngham Plunket in June 1863, Benjamin Lee gave her away at a ceremony in Clontarf, performed by Lord Plunket, Bishop of Tuam and uncle to the groom. In the city, the bells of St Patrick's pealed in celebration, answered by the bells of Christ Church. Once the marriage was complete, everyone piled back to St Anne's, where Benjamin Lee threw a gorgeous wedding breakfast in superb surroundings. The report in the *Dublin Evening Mail* gives a glimpse not just of 'Marriage in High Life', as they head-lined the piece, but of the interior of St Anne's.

> The hall and banqueting rooms, enriched with rare and valuable pictures, statuary, and other art treasures, were decorated with the choicest flowers and exotics and looked magnificent, while from the windows were to be observed charming combinations of exquisite landscape gardening, and views of mountain, wood, and water.

The 'monster bride cake' was made by Mitchell's, a fashionable bakery, confectionery and coffee shop at 10 Grafton Street, just across the Green. The richly decorated cake weighed 140 lbs, making it riskier than usual to hold it 'over the bride's head according to the old custom', but this was nonetheless done, before the giant cake was cut and portioned out among the guests. Following another tradition, the 'numerous and valuable' wedding presents were laid out for the guests to admire. The Dean of St Patrick's had given 'a massive gold bracelet, bearing a large oval amethyst', while the Guinness workers had clubbed together to give a large clock made by Elkington of College Green. After all the appropriate toasts, the newly married couple set off for the boat at Kingstown to start the first leg of their honeymoon trip to Switzerland.

The family dynamic was changing as the years passed. In January of the same year, Arthur II's 'Beloved Arthur Lee', Benjamin Lee's brother, had died, unmarried to the last and leaving no will to direct what would happen to his modest estate of under £4,000. Now Benjamin Lee's eldest child was married. Meanwhile, his youngest, Edward Cecil, was working in the brewery, though he had not completely set aside his education, and was still studying away with the aim of entering Trinity.

In 1865 Benjamin Lee's two big Dublin projects came to fruition: the reopening of St Patrick's and the Great Exhibition. As far as the cathedral restoration went, the original £30,000 was nowhere near the final figure, but, true to his word, Benjamin Lee settled the bill for everything, closing out at £150,000. The Dublin building firm Murphy's of Amiens Street carried out the works to completion, and in February 1865 the cathedral was ready to be used again as originally intended.

On a cool, sunny morning, 2,000 people attended the first service in the restored cathedral. Among them, Benjamin Lee took his seat, accompanied by Anne, now Mrs Plunket, and two of his sons, Arthur Edward and Lee, as well as Frederick Darley. Edward Cecil was not there that day, nor was Elizabeth, who perhaps had not felt well enough for the short journey from St Stephen's Green, even to see her husband's work so gloriously finished. The following month, the Lord Mayor gave a banquet for Benjamin Lee to acknowledge his service in underwriting the restoration. It was an all-male evening for 80 guests, so Elizabeth was not at it, but she was on her husband's arm for the ball thrown for the Prince of Wales at Dublin's Mansion House in May.

The prince came over to Ireland for the opening of the exhibition in May and stayed in Dublin for three days. He arrived without his wife, Alexandra of Denmark, now the Princess of Wales since their marriage in March 1863. Elizabeth Guinness might have been hoping for a glimpse of the princess, if not an introduction: she had been on the committee that organised the royal wedding gift 'from the ladies of Ireland', in the form of 'a complete set of the most beautiful lace our Island can produce'. But the prince travelled alone, and as his coach passed from Kingstown through the city centre to the Viceregal Lodge in the Phoenix Park, 'the crowds were immense, and the reception if not tremendous in its enthusiasm, was at least unmarred by the slightest indication of an unpleasant sort', in the words of the *Scotsman*, which sounded like damning with faint praise, but was at least an acknowledgement that not everyone in Dublin was delighted to have a royal visit.

Dublin generally dazzled through the press reports. St Stephen's Green, Edward Cecil's playground, was a 'splendid square, unequalled in the empire'; and at the opening ceremony in the Exhibition Palace, 'on every side, wherever the eye could travel, the attention was attested by one sight more beautiful and impressive than another'. Conditions around the Green were imperfect, as the dry ground resulted in cloud after cloud of dust being thrown up by thousands of carriage wheels, and – as was to be expected at an event of this size – a great press began outside the gates long before the appointed opening time.

Those with season tickets were assured of entry but did not have reserved seating, and they were 'desirous at all hazards to secure good seats ... the rush, on the opening was consequently extreme and somewhat destructive to the dress of those who shared in it'. But these quibbles were just indicators of the vivid attraction of the exhibition and the fact that the opening had been a topic of conversation in the capital for weeks on end. Everyone wanted to see inside. Benjamin Lee was on the Reception Committee, headed by the Lord Chancellor, that conducted the prince to the dais erected for the royal party.

That night Benjamin Lee and Elizabeth, along with Lee and Edward Cecil, as well as Frederick Darley, dressed in their best clothes and crossed the Green to Dawson Street and the ball given by the Lord Mayor for the prince. About 2,000 people were there – more like 3,000 in the estimate of the *Irish Times* – and as the weather, ever capricious, had turned from dry to wet, the carriages with ladies in them all had to stop under the awning of the Mansion House.

This caused a bottleneck from both directions, and some guests had to spend more hours of the evening than they would have liked sitting impatiently in their carriages, straining to hear the music and to see who was getting out of the carriages ahead. Inside 'it was impossible to avoid crushing at times', even though the Round Room had been supplemented with a suite of other rooms, so it can't have been a hugely comfortable atmosphere for Elizabeth if she was still feeling unwell or tired. Unlike the Lord Mayor's event in March, when Benjamin Lee was the most honoured guest, tonight he was only one of hundreds of important guests, preceded by hundreds of very important ones. A string band played waltzes, galops, quadrilles and lancers, and the dancing continued into the early hours of the morning, even long after the prince's departure for the Viceregal Lodge at two in the morning.

In terms of profit, the 1865 exhibition showed only £10,000, and even this figure was subsequently disputed as being far too high. But as a spectacle, and as a showcase, it had been a triumph. An initial report showed that it had brought in 930,000 visitors by the time the turnstiles closed in November, and it was the talk of the town both in the run-up to and throughout that glorious summer and autumn.

It had taken a huge amount of effort to produce. Those celebratory civic occasions in the spring and early summer of 1865, the public face of much private work, decision-making, discussion and planning, were among the last of the great events that Benjamin Lee would be able to chat about with Elizabeth, his wife, cousin and 'own sweet Love'. 'Poor Mother is very weak but slept well,' wrote Edward Cecil to his brother Lee, and indeed Elizabeth was weakening.

She lived to see her husband elected an MP that July, but she died two months later, aged only 51. Her funeral was held on 27 September, her body taken from St Anne's in a suite of coffins of cedar, lead and polished oak, with the exterior coffin mounted in black forest oak and brass. As well as the immediate family mourners there was a string of other Guinnesses, friends and associates. Benjamin Lee entered this new and final phase of his life, as a widower – and an MP living in London.

Sectional view of the Storehouse at St James's Gate,
from *Midland Railway Guide*, 1867.

SEVEN

INHERITANCE

While Benjamin Lee was spending hand over fist on these huge civic projects, as well as on his own property portfolio, he had not ignored the brewery. Anything but. In the years after his father's death Benjamin Lee had not only switched up the splendour of his lifestyle in town and country, embarked on a programme of public works and – free of paternal remonstrances – become an MP. Once he finally came into his own, he tripled the size of the brewery site and pushed its expansion and production, so that by the time he died, it was in the extraordinary position of being the largest brewery in the world.

Benjamin Lee had so many interests to look after outside the brewery, but he still kept a close eye on it. As time passed, and he grew older, he could excusably have removed himself into a role of oversight and remained at a greater distance from the minutiae of brewing than his father or his grandfather had. But he did not choose this path, perhaps because a life of absorption in the detail had left him uneasy operating more remotely.

He had a solid manager *in situ*, in the form of John Tertius Purser, whose father and grandfather had become partners in the firm in 1820. Tertius himself did not want a partnership, but his great experience and skill were crucial in managing the business. The long association with the Purser family, and the careful tending of the relationships through the generations of Guinnesses and Pursers, had paid off in spades. Things were not always cordial, naturally enough, but everybody involved was playing a long game, and knew it. John Purser Junior (the second generation) kept an intermittent diary, in which, 37 years into his career at the brewery, he noted a day in 1837 when Arthur II was 'haughty', though he also noted the subsequent apology. There were clashes of character and approach, and when another Guinness, John, left the brewery the same year, Purser described it as a comfort to Tertius (the third generation), whose temper and manner improved when he no longer had to work with someone with whom he didn't get on.

In 1840, just after Arthur Lee had left the brewery, it seems that John Purser Junior sought something more from the partnership agreement. Arthur II wrote to him: 'I confess that on one or two occasions there was a coldness and dissatisfaction manifested in your manner towards me which I felt I did not deserve at your hands.' It suggests that each side was capable of sensitivity to the manner of the other, though Arthur describes his reaction as 'momentary, as I am not in the habit of retaining in my mind feelings of the kind', while Purser, a man who felt things deeply, perhaps dwelt for longer on an analysis of the relationship. He felt that it was to his and his son's disadvantage to have been known more or less as children,

> and we are regarded too often as children still ... I was young and could be contrould [sic] I was poor and could be patronised – but not now either liking controul [sic] or desiring patronage I am looked upon with less favourable eyes.

Purser's frustrated private musings did not always tally with what he expressed elsewhere. Fundamentally, like anyone, he wanted to feel valued, and when he was sent to London in November 1843 and committed a hefty £25,000 of the firm's money to the purchase of hops, he was 'well pleased to see that my care caution and judgment were marked with the approbation of my partners'. When Benjamin Lee was Lord Mayor of Dublin in 1851, he invited John Purser to a dinner, and Purser's emotional thank-you letter far exceeded a standard acknowledgement note:

> God has indeed been very gracious to me in placing me when yet a child under the care and instruction of your

excellent father and now an old man I feel proud of your
good opinion and blessed and happy in the possession of
your confidence.

Purser had been the oldest person present at the banquet, and
had known both Benjamin Lee and his father longer than anyone
else had. Purser said he knew 'more of your minds and thoughts
than all who sat at meat with you', and asked pardon for 'the
garrulity of an old man who feels himself indebted for years
of continuing and unending kindness'. The Guinnesses always
wrote of the Pursers in affectionate terms, and recognised theirs
as capable hands. John Purser Junior noted with satisfaction that
three generations of Pursers had made long and profitable careers
at St James's Gate, and 'our promotion has been the result of
our own character and faithfulness'. He was right, and after his
death in 1858, his son John Tertius was able to mentor the young
Guinness brothers Arthur and Edward Cecil.

Knowing this, and with the brewery now expanded, on a
solid financial footing and under wise management, Benjamin
Lee was able to turn his mind to standing for election, something
from which he had up to now shied away. The possibility had
first been raised in 1851, but his father had strongly advised him
against it, on the grounds of it being 'fraught with difficulty and
danger' in circumstances where Dublin had been riven with party
politics and the religious divide. It would have created an even
worse situation 'if filled by one engaged in our line of business'.

Benjamin Lee had been happy enough to follow his father's
direction at that time, but by 1865 the political situation in Dublin
felt calmer and the brewery steadier. He stood as a Conservative
in the Dublin City seat vacated when the Conservative MP Sir
Edward Grogan retired, and, as the *Illustrated London News* put
it, 'Mr Benjamin Guinness ... was returned, very naturally, with
the good-will of all parties', to a house with an increased Liberal
majority under the leadership of Lord Palmerston. The timing
would turn out to be fortunate for Benjamin Lee, as Elizabeth's

death would follow so quickly after the election. Losing her was hard to bear, and as a politician Benjamin Lee would at least have the distraction of a completely different project to engage his never-idle brain.

The second Dublin City seat was won by Jonathan Pim, for the Liberal Party. Pim belonged to a Quaker merchant family in the textile business, and Pim Brothers in South Great George's Street was one of Dublin's first department stores. His sibling Thomas Pim had worked with Benjamin Lee as a co-director of the Dublin Exhibition Palace and Winter Garden Company. Jonathan Pim and Benjamin Lee Guinness stood for different parties, but, Pim said, they together represented 'the moderate men of all parties'.

The morning the election results were to be declared, people crammed into the courthouse at Green Street to hear the tallies called by the High Sheriff of Dublin, who, to whoops and cheers and waving of handkerchiefs and hats, declared Mr Guinness elected with 4,739 votes, and Mr Pim elected with 4,635. Benjamin Lee got to his feet to speak, and, in a rare recorded error, said, 'You have elected me and my friend Mr Vance', Vance being the other Conservative candidate, defeated by Pim. 'The scene of uproar, groaning, hissing, hooting and bahing that here ensured it would be impossible to describe,' noted the reporter for the *Dublin Evening Post*.

Mr Guinness, MP, resumed: There is an old saying—
A Voice: Next to heart next to mind.
Mr Guinness: Well, there is an old saying that Irish ladies are allowed to answer twice, and that they are not held responsible for what they first say. I do not know whether I may ask the same favour on the part of an Irish gentle-man, for although I mentioned that name I intended to speak of my friend, Mr Pim.
A Voice: We forgive you now that you disown Vance *(cheers)*.

It is an unusual little vignette. The typical picture we have of Benjamin Lee is of a man in control of any situation he found himself in, from the detail of a hop order or a clerk's pay rise to the management of an international export operation. There is something touchingly and fundamentally human about this 67-year-old man who, in a crowded, noisy courtroom, finds that he is to embark on a new career as an MP and, in the excitement and heat of the moment, fumbles his words. Immediately, he drew the crowd back to himself, allowing space for the heckling, regaining the approval of the room with reference to an old familiar saying, and praising the popular Pim to his supporters. We do hear old family voices through letters, diaries, legal documents and, in some cases, prepared public speeches, but it is precious and rare to hear them speaking spontaneously.

Something else he remarked on that day was that the conduct of the election had been peaceful and orderly and a model of fair play. Dublin was now in a peaceable state, but Benjamin Lee well remembered, he said, the time when 'the immortal Henry Grattan was pelted through the streets of Dublin, and when he had to fly into a house in Henry street to escape'. Given Grattan was well known to Benjamin Lee's grandparents Arthur I and Olivia, that memory must have been particularly vivid. Every living Guinness remembered or knew about the violent attacks on brewery customers and delivery men 30 years earlier, and Benjamin Lee certainly remembered his father's specific warning 15 years previously, so perhaps cross-party co-operation in a city with more concord felt all the sweeter and all the more promising.

Being an MP meant moving to London for at least a portion of the year, and for Benjamin Lee this meant his Mayfair house, 27 Norfolk Street (now called Dunraven Street). As MPs he and Pim worked on various matters together, including the introduction of improved regulation for stockbrokers, one of the last issues he dealt with, but the two also voted in opposition to one another from time to time.

In the spring of 1867, another late transition occurred, with the establishment's approbation: a baronetcy. Benjamin Lee was the most successful businessman in Ireland, generous and wide-ranging in his philanthropy, civic-minded and now politically active. 'The Governor', as his children called him, now became Sir Benjamin Lee Guinness, Bart, MP, his seat Ashford Castle. He was also now entitled to bear supporters to his arms. These 'supporters' are figures on either side of the shield device on a coat of arms, exemplified in the lion and the unicorn on the British royal coat of arms. A letter to Sir Benjamin from Bernard Burke at Dublin Castle, the same Burke of *Burke's Peerage* and *Burke's Landed Gentry*, opened:

> Our wished for object is now attained. It is Her Majesty's pleasure that you and each of your Successors in the Baronetcy shall have the high honor and distinction of Supporters to your arms. The College Heralds in London will now complete the good work, well and speedily I trust.

However thrilled Sir Benjamin was for himself and for Arthur, who as the eldest son would inherit the baronetcy as well as so much on the material side, he didn't enjoy it for long. It was late in life to be kicking off a political career, and the novelty and stimulation of the House of Commons and the pleasures of London palled in fairly short order. When fatigue and ill-health prevailed Sir Benjamin longed for the dear familiar rhythms of life at home at St Anne's.

Edward Cecil brought him down to the Queen's Hotel in Sydenham, Kent in May 1868, and wrote from there to his elder brother Arthur that their father was 'very weak and languid, his stomach is very much out of order, he thinks caused by want of exercise which his cold prevented him taking'. He was 'heartily sick of London, and of being a member [of Parliament]'. Edward Cecil accompanied his father back to Mayfair the next day, and reported to Arthur that he was 'exceedingly weak today and very sickish', adding that, despite this weakness, 'the Devil can't induce him to see a doctor'. He had lost all appetite and was eating barely anything.

He did, however, at last consent to be seen by a doctor, who identified bronchitis and recommended that he go back to Ireland, to the west, which meant Ashford. However, Benjamin Lee had decided that he wanted to be present for a House of Commons vote on franchise reform and so would stay on in London for another two days, despite his hand shaking so much that Edward Cecil had to sign a letter for him. The next letter was followed hastily by a telegram, calling Arthur Edward over to London. Sir Benjamin died the following Tuesday, 19 May, and his sons brought him home to Ireland to be buried.

As was obvious to anyone who read a paper or walked the streets of Dublin, Benjamin Lee Guinness had become steadily richer and richer as his porter's popularity reached across the nation and then the world. He and his family lived in unmistakeable style, in beautiful houses well maintained and gorgeously decorated, filled with paintings and sculptures. Teams of servants at St Stephen's Green, St Anne's and Ashford Castle raked out ashes and laid fires, heated water, laundered, pressed and mended clothes, swept and polished the floors, and many times every day prepared and cooked food, then washed, dried and put away the glasses, plates, pots and silverware.

Outside, more workers kept the gardens in good order, looked after the horses and maintained the carriages. The family spent time in England and in France, in ones and twos and all together, and they made education as much a priority as apprenticeship to business. Benjamin Lee began his life in great comfort, but by the end was living in what can only be described as luxury. However, this luxury was restrained both by taste and morality, tempered by the sobriety of the Protestant middle-class and a constant awareness of one's Christian duty.

The Guinness children's lives were mingled with their parents'; they were taught charity as well as faith, and went to work at an early age. Days were bookended by prayers, family breakfasts and six o'clock dinners, with church on Sundays non-negotiable, and daily exercise taken for granted. This was Sir Benjamin's approach to good living. Although everyone knew he was rich, it was only when he died that the full extent of his wealth became apparent. The Irish probate system had never seen such a fortune: his estate amounted to £1,100,000, his will the largest ever proved in the country.

He left his estates in the west of Ireland and the family home at St Anne's to Arthur Edward, now suddenly Sir Arthur. His Kerry, Limerick and Kilkenny estates, with £20,000, went to Lee, now a captain in the 1st Life Guards. No. 80 was to be Edward Cecil's, along with the trust fund created from Elizabeth's marriage settlement, and £10,000 to complete the lease of property and mills in Kilmainham, west of St James's Gate. There was £30,000 to be allocated for investment to benefit Annie, now and until her father-in-law's death the Hon. Mrs Plunket. Sir Benjamin had drafted his will in a manner that showed his particular intention to safeguard the interests of the brewery, almost as if it were a fifth child. He directed it to be passed to Arthur Edward and Edward Cecil, for them to carry it on together. In order to keep the brewery capitalised, he specified that, if one brother wanted out or was declared bankrupt, then his share passed to the other.

The will was thus remarkably unequal in its treatment of Sir Benjamin's four grown-up children, but he seems to have taken the circumstances, preferences and foreseeable future of each into account. Edward Cecil, though the youngest, had always had a strong bond with his father; he had entered the brewery at 15, developed relationships with the senior staff and the Pursers, and shown not only suitability but eagerness to drive the whole operation. Sir Benjamin had had the advantage for almost all his life of having his father alive to advise and direct him, and he knew that, because he was an older father – he had already turned 40 by the time his first child, Annie Lee, was born – his own children would not have that luxury.

Nor had his children the same proximity to the founding of the brewery. Benjamin Lee was only five when his grandfather Arthur died, but he grew up absorbing an understanding of what it had taken to build the business, and taking nothing for granted. Annie, Arthur, Lee and Edward had been born into a very different environment, with plenty of money, a selection of luxurious houses, a steady social position, and an ever more elevated circle of friends and connections. Naturally enough, any Guinness child knew where the money was coming from, but it didn't necessarily mean much to them, as a charming memory recounted by Edward Cecil's grandson Bryan Guinness shows. He wrote of the

> misconception that arose from my father saying as we drove past the Brewery in Dublin: 'That's where the bread-and-butter comes from.' I can't be sure how long I believed that the place produced bread-and-butter. I fancy that my grandfather may have said the same thing when my father was a child.

As the eldest son, Arthur Edward would all his life have had certain expectations: that Ashford Castle would be his, and all those who worked there would become his responsibility; that the brewery would be his, in whole or in part; and, in the year before his father's death, this view of the future had come to include inheriting the new baronetcy. Unlike his youngest brother, as a child he was sent away to school at Eton, though the Eton Register lists him as having lasted only a year, leaving in 1853 when still only 13. Boarding-school life and culture may not have suited him, but he was undoubtedly bright and curious, and went on to study at Trinity. There he mingled his academic work and sitting for examinations with going to receptions at the Viceregal Lodge and spending time in the brewery.

But Arthur Edward's real interest was in politics, and of course one thing his father left was an empty seat in the House of Commons. Arthur pleased the Dublin electorate and he quickly filled the seat, though it was only a few months before Disraeli called a general election and the new Liberals were returned with a majority. Gladstone embarked on his first premiership, and Arthur briefly entered the opposition. Arthur's early political career was tainted by charges of corruption, and exactly what this meant for the rest of his political life, and how it all played out with the brewery partnership, will be considered in the next chapter.

The army career of the second son, Lee, had effectively ruled him out of the brewery. He may already have ruled himself out on other grounds, though, as he had got himself into some financial trouble early on, and been dug out by his father. Even with the property, £20,000 was a modest enough legacy and suggests that Lee had already seen significant benefit during his father's lifetime. The phrasing of the bequest was highly directional:

> I do earnestly and affectionately enjoin on my said dear son not to expend any portion of the said sum of £20,000 thus placed at his disposal save for the purpose of purchasing military promotion or of eventually settling himself in some civil occupation should he leave the military service or in the purchase of real estates.

The £30,000 in trust for Anne did not come with such strictures. Lee did leave military service, as his father seems to have suspected he might, after reaching the rank of captain, but he didn't settle into any civil occupation, unless you count country gentleman. Martelli found that the only record of his taking any interest in the brewery was 'that for a short period he took it into his head to superintend the internal management and got as far as designing a uniform for the employees, but "quickly tired of the work which proved uncongenial to him"', and indeed it must have been exhausting. In 1881 Lee married Lady Henrietta St Lawrence, a daughter of the Earl of Howth.

Annie had nothing to do with the brewery either. At that time no woman did, in any capacity. She was born in 1839, shortly after the family moved to St Anne's, and to celebrate her birth, Benjamin Lee, bursting with paternal pride, built a tower bridge over the entrance drive, and although the house is no longer there, the Annie Lee Bridge is still standing in what is now St Anne's Park.

Like Edward Cecil, as a youngster Annie frequently found herself walking with her father around Dublin city centre, in particular the Liberties, where she observed the deprivation and difficulties experienced by the community. In 1860, the Halls described the textile industry traditional to the Liberties, an area they found impoverished and neglected. They remarked on the success of Guinness porter, not just in Ireland but worldwide:

> The other manufactures that flourish in Dublin, unhappily, require but a very brief notice … ; the porter, if we may class it under this head, of Messrs. Guinness is preferred to that of any other brewery in all parts of the world. The amount of its consumption in London alone is immense.

So, another excellent mention for the brewery, but there wasn't much else to impress the Halls, who also noticed that the rich of the city had migrated from the west of the city, where the brewery and the Liberties lay, towards the east, abandoning the large houses, grand staircases and corniced rooms which they had once filled with fine furniture, artworks and the sons and daughters of privilege.

> They are now the abode only of the most miserable. As they were deserted by the rich, they were filled by the poor; and as they decayed, they became the resort of the more abject, who could find no other shelter. So crowded were they at one time, that 108 persons were found in one house lying on the bare floor, and in one room seven out of twelve were labouring under typhus fever.

As was the way all around Dublin, poverty lived cheek by jowl with opulence, and within yards of St Stephen's Green Annie Lee saw it for herself, as her youngest brother did. The enormous amounts of money being spent on the cathedral were pouring into the heart of a community struggling with want, poor housing and illness. The newspapers wrote columns and columns about it. A few months before Annie's wedding, in the spring of 1863, the *Freeman's Journal* wrote:

> Were it not for the benevolent operation of the Sick and Indigent Roomkeepers' Society, the St Vincent de Paul's Society, and some local relief associations the poor would have been thrown into a pitiable condition; but these societies, with the limited means at their disposal, can never grapple with the great emergency of the present crisis ... there is more absolute destitution and sickness in the Coombe, New Market, Meath-street, Pimlico, Tripoli, Cole-alley, Vicar-street, Engine-alley, Brabazon-street, Braithwaite-street, Elbow-lane, Plunkett-street, and Hanover-lane than could in former years be found in the entire city.

The South Dublin Union workhouse was packed to the rafters, and its hospital could take no more of the sick poor, even though a variation of typhoid fever was doing the rounds, and the systems of the 'famishing poor' had little to no resistance to illness. The streets named in the newspaper report all lay in the small section of city between St Stephen's Green and the brewery, and would have been home to at least some of the brewery labourers.

The archive of brewery employment records preserved today shows, just by way of example, that a James Toole worked as a labourer in the brewhouse from March 1863, and lived at 42 Meath Street. James Murphy, a labourer in the cooperage department, lived 13 houses away at number 55, a few men lived on the Coombe, and one in Braithwaite Street. So these streets, in the news for such unusual levels of poverty and deprivation, were geographically close to home for Annie Lee: they formed part of the cityscape she walked with her father, they housed members of the church and cathedral congregation, and were home to men who worked for her family business.

Unfortunately, they also formed the same community for the relief of whose poverty Annie Lee's great-grandfather and the brewery founder, Arthur Guinness, had formed a committee in 1793. This was the committee for the relief of the manufacturing poor because 'adequate relief cannot at present be obtained', and Arthur, along with his fellow church-warden, and the vicar of St Catherine's church, had entreated people to

> contribute their friendly aid, in order to enable them to relieve their suffering fellow creatures, and alleviate in some degree, that misery and wretchedness which are ever attendant on hunger and want, and afford them the means of giving succour to the disconsolate, helpless and forsaken wife, and the more desolate, pining, innocent children!

In the 1860s, 70 years later, these communities were still struggling. As a Guinness, Annie Lee was constitutionally disposed to identify charitable causes with personal resonance, and as she contemplated her own marriage and future, this meant mothers and children. When still Annie Lee Guinness, and still only 23, she drummed up volunteers to form a committee, and dedicated a small legacy of her own to funding several useful local initiatives. Chief among these was a project to introduce a 'Bible-woman'. The Bible-woman was, in the missionary tradition, someone who could offer spiritual guidance through the scriptures, but also did a combination of listening, counselling and social work, to the extent of their time and resources. There were Bible-women associated with the Bethesda chapel, with St Catherine's in Thomas Street and with the Dublin City Mission at Merchants' Hall.

Annie Lee, even after she became the Hon. Mrs Conyngham, and subsequently Lady Plunket, never wavered in her commitment to finding ways to improve the lives of mothers and children in the Liberties. She and her committee were soon in a position to provide a district nurse as well as the Bible-woman, and in 1876 founded St Patrick's Home for Nursing the Sick Poor, and later St Patrick's Nurses' Home.

Close to Annie's heart was the Mothers' Meeting, which she instigated in 1865. A handful of women, half a dozen at most, turned up to its first few sessions in a borrowed room, but the idea caught the breeze. Women wanted it. By 1879 there were five Mothers' Meeting branches, one of which was attached to St Patrick's Cathedral and drew about 150 women to its Tuesday morning meeting. By now there were seven Bible-women, three Nurses and more than 50 District Visitors at work in the quarter, not just dispensing Bible stories as a balm for the day's anxieties, but also doing the highly practical work of teaching needlework and other skills, giving advice, lending books and administering blanket and coal funds.

The activities were incorporated into the Dublin Women's Work Association, endorsed and supported by the ecclesiastical hierarchy. This included Annie's husband William, who initially with his father-in-law's help had become treasurer and then precentor of St Patrick's, and went on to become Bishop of Meath, and then Archbishop of Dublin in 1884. Lord Plunket, as he became, had a liberal outlook, illustrated in a letter to Annie in 1876 in which he said he 'could have wept' when the Church of Ireland Synod 'defeated an attempt which some of us were making to allow a poor unbaptized infant to be buried with some other burial than that of a dog'. Though he claimed to be undemonstrative, he clearly adored his wife, and was proud of the work she undertook. As archbishop, he addressed a drawing-room meeting of the association in the Bishop's Palace in St Stephen's Green. Everyone who needed aid should have it, regardless of religion.

Lord Plunket was at pains to stress that the association was not a proselytising organisation, and that its workers were not precluded from speaking what they believed to be the truth, but that their primary object was the temporal and spiritual welfare of the poorer members of the Protestant church. He acknowledged

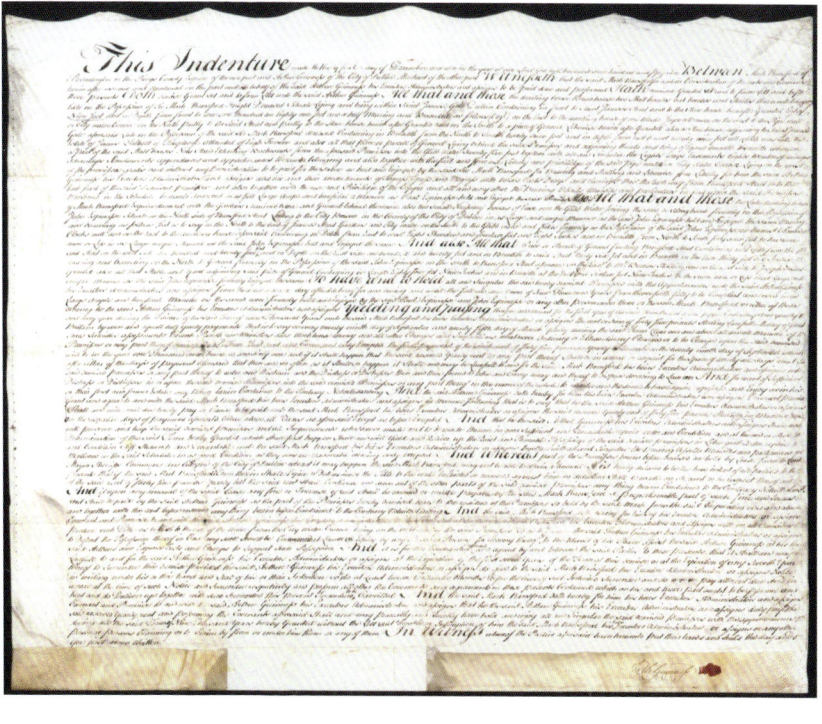

Top: Our family portraits of the first Arthur Guinness, who founded the brewery in St James's Gate in 1759; and his wife Olivia Whitmore, with whom he had 21 children.

Bottom: The original 9,000-year lease for the Guinness brewery at St James's Gate in Dublin, dated 1759 and signed by Arthur Guinness at bottom right.

Top left: The author with a statue of the first Arthur Guinness in Celbridge, Co. Kildare, where Arthur grew up.

Top right: Grave of Arthur and Olivia Guinness in Oughterard Church.

Left: A page from the Minute Book of the Brewers' Guild of Dublin from 1766, which records Arthur being elected as Master of the Guild.

Top: The Guinness brewery viewed through its entrance on James's Street, *c.*1840.

Bottom: Aquatint and etching by Robert Havell the Younger (after Joseph Patrick Haverty), depicting the departure from Dun Laoghaire of George IV on 3 September 1821. During the king's trip to Dublin, Arthur Guinness II had shown him around the Bank of Ireland, and he was at Dun Laoghaire (along with Daniel O'Connell) as part of the deputation to see him off – a mark of how far the Guinness family had already come in one generation.

Four family portraits. *Anticlockwise from top right:* The second Arthur Guinness, painted by J.C. Miles; Arthur's wife, Anne Lee; their second son, Arthur Lee; and their third son, Benjamin Lee Guinness (painted by Stephen Catterson Smith), who inherited the brewery in 1855, having been a full partner in it since 1820.

Top: The Guinness brewery at St James's Gate, in a sketch from the earliest guidebook depicting it, the *Midland Railway Guide* of 1867.

Bottom: One of the earliest known photographs of the St James's Gate brewery, showing the Brewhouse in the front yard, *c.*1885–87.

Top: Portrait of Benjamin Lee Guinness with his two of his children, my great-great-grandfather Edward Cecil (left) and Annie, *c.*1850s.

Left: Vintage photograph of John Henry Foley's statue of Sir Benjamin Lee Guinness, posthumously erected outside St Patrick's Cathedral, Dublin in 1875 in recognition of the cathedral renovations that he had funded and directed.

Opposite top: Elizabeth Guinness with their two other children, Arthur (left) and Lee, *c.*1845.

Opposite bottom: A pencil sketch of Arthur, later 1st Baron Ardilaun, and a photograph of Edward Cecil (Ned), later 1st Earl of Iveagh. The two brothers ran the brewery together from 1868 until 1876, when Ned bought out Arthur.

ST. PATRICK'S CATHL. DUBLIN. 63 W.L.

Top: Dublin's International Exhibition of 1865, in a print published in the *Illustrated London News*. Benjamin Lee Guinness was a trustee of the exhibition and provided its site in Coburg Gardens, behind his St Stephen's Green home. Nearly a million people visited it that year.

Bottom: St Patrick's Cathedral, Dublin, with St Patrick's Park in the foreground. A generation after the cathedral was restored by Benjamin Lee Guinness, this public park was cleared and laid out by the Iveagh Trust with funding by Ned Guinness.

Top: The Guinness brewery was always keen to adopt new technology. In the 1870s it built a narrow-gauge railway to carry raw materials around the site and deliver full casks of beer down to the river for shipping further afield.

Bottom: Photochrome print of St Stephen's Green, the largest of Dublin's Georgian garden squares, *c.*1890s. Arthur, Lord Ardilaun, funded the park's purchase, transformed it through landscaping and planting, and gave it to the city as a green space for those without their own gardens.

Top: 80–81 St Stephen's Green, Dublin, the grand family residence bought by Benjamin Lee Guinness and inherited by Ned Guinness. It was later gifted to the Irish state. Today, renamed Iveagh House, it houses the Department of Foreign Affairs.

Left: Photograph of the interior staircase at 80–81 St Stephen's Green, on a page in Ned's family album, signed on 17 April 1899 by the Duke and Duchess of York (later George V and Queen Mary) during their visit. Ned had escorted them around the brewery too.

Top left: Adelaide Guinness, photographed as ever in profile, with 'Wolf', her Irish wolf hound, 1896.

Top right: Portrait of Edward Cecil Guinness by Henry Marriott Paget after the original by Arthur Stockdale Cope, after 1912. Ned wears the blue sash and star of the Order of St Patrick. When he was made a Knight of St Patrick, his brother Arthur's feathers were ruffled.

Bottom: Ned and Adelaide's three sons, Rupert, Ernest and Walter, outside Farmleigh, probably in the late 1890s.

Top: The October 1896 shooting party at Elveden. Back row: Judith Harbord, Lionel Sackville-West, Lord Suffield, Derek Keppel, Adelaide, Lord Rowton, Ned, William Waldorf Astor. Middle row: Lady Morris, Victoria Sackville-West, Lady Granby, Lord Morris, Lady Bantry. Front row: Margaret Kerr-Pearse, Lord Granby, Lord Rathmore, Norah Oldfield.

Bottom left: Duleep Singh, the deposed Maharaja of the Punjab, painted by Franz Xaver Winterhalter in 1854 when the sitter was 15. He owned Elveden Hall; after his death, it was bought and extended by Ned Guinness.

Bottom right: Drawing Room at Elveden, with Mughal-style marble interiors originally commissioned by Duleep Singh, furnished by Ned and Adelaide Guinness, *c.*late 1890s.

A telling page from the family album: a shooting party at Elveden in December 1901, with guests including the future George V (at the wheel of the car on the left). Ned stands at far left; Ernest is seated in front of him; Adelaide is above the Prince, in profile; Rupert kneels at the centre. The photograph is juxtaposed with a sketch of 'Dublin Street Children' added to the same page; the Guinnesses did not forget those at home needing help.

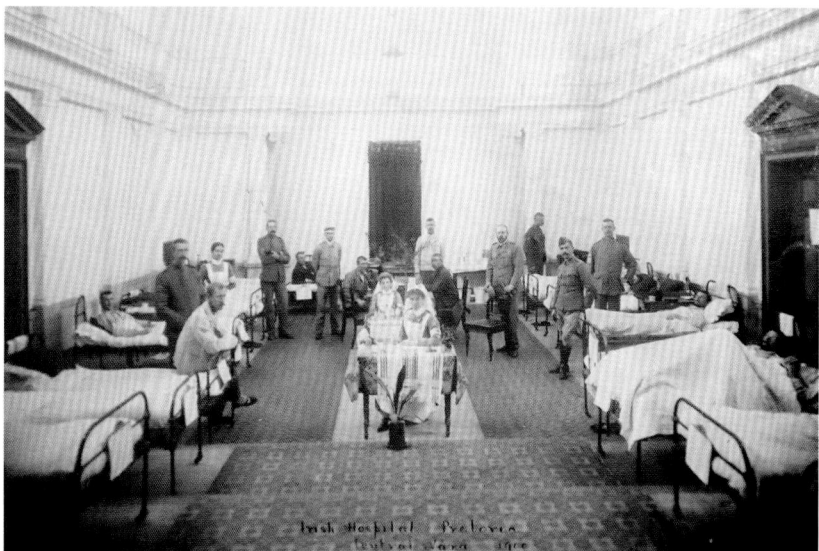

Top: The Lister Institute of Preventive Medicine in London, part-funded by Ned Guinness.

Bottom: Central Ward at the Irish Hospital in Pretoria, 1900. Ned funded it, and his son Rupert Guinness (my great-grandfather) served here during the Boer War.

Opposite: Three buildings provided for the people of Dublin by the munificence of Ned Guinness and the Iveagh Trust: (top) the Iveagh Play Centre; (middle) the Iveagh Markets building; (bottom) Edward VII arrives at the Iveagh Trust buildings, 1903.

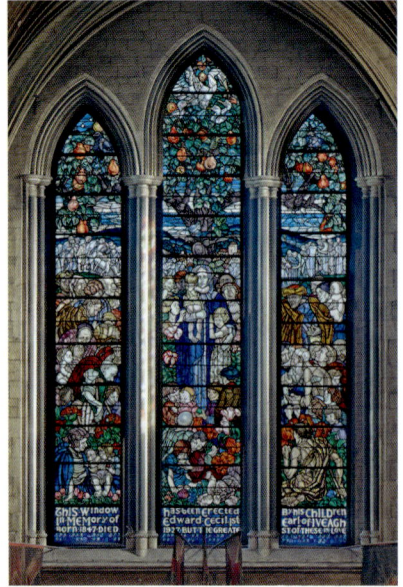

Top left: Ned, 1st Earl of Iveagh, photographed by Walter Stoneman in 1926, the year before his death.

Top right: The Iveagh Window at St Patrick's Cathedral, designed by Sir Frank Brangwyn, represents Charity ministering to suffering humanity, and commemorates Ned, who, like his father, had funded renovations to the cathedral.

Left: The author looking out over Elveden's central marble hall, summer 2025.

and admired the work being done by the Catholic orders, particularly the Sisters of Charity and the Sisters of Mercy, and felt that the women of the Dublin Women's Work Association were a kind of Protestant Sisters of Charity. This praise was possibly overblown, but it does show how passionately and publicly the archbishop supported his wife's work.

Lady Plunket was a 'sweet and gentle hostess', one friend wrote of a visit to the Bishop's Palace at Ardbraccan, while another described her as 'at all times given to hospitality ... she remembered with a tact peculiarly her own the personal tastes of her guests. So cordial as well as personal was the welcome, that each one had the gratifying sense of being individually considered' – and this in a house that could sleep 61 people. But one morning during the visit it rained and the temperature dropped, leaving Lady Plunket 'tortured by neuralgia and unable to leave her room'.

She had been unwell in one way or another from the early years of her marriage, meaning she had often had to go abroad for various cures and changes of climate, and when she died in 1889 she was only 50, even younger than her mother had been. She passed away at home, Old Connaught House, Bray, leaving six children as well as her widower. Her death certificate attributed her end to chronic hepatitis and multiple neuritis.

Annie Lee Plunket was by all accounts a cheerful, attractive, light-hearted person. She was deeply religious and carried her beliefs into her daily life, working to improve the lives of individuals, and of the community that surrounded the newly magnificent St Patrick's, and later funnelling her energy into the Clergy Daughters' School in Earlsfort Terrace. Hers was a quiet, patient philanthropy. Benjamin Lee knew that, as William Conyngham's wife, she would have love, security and material comfort, and she did. Could Annie Lee have done with a greater share of her father's enormous estate? Perhaps. The woman who was once left £25 to buy herself a ring, and instead invested it in charity, was unlikely to have wanted it for herself. But she might well have made wise investments on others' behalf.

The three brothers Guinness: Edward Cecil, Arthur and Lee.

EIGHT

THE BROTHERS GUINNESS

Two young men now co-owned the largest porter brewery in the world. How was it all going to work out? The brothers got on well enough, but their relationship had not yet been tested in the commercial environment. Arthur was the older brother, and now Sir Arthur to Edward Cecil's plain Master Guinness. Edward Cecil wasn't even 21 when their father died, and Arthur therefore might have expected to have more of a say in things than his younger brother, still a minor, still at university.

Yet these two of the siblings, at least, had been treated equally by their father's will; the brewery was now held by both in equal share. For all his youth, Edward Cecil had already spent almost six years working in the business. He was quick, sharp and decisive, and he had the same head for detail that had characterised each of the brewery owners to date. Perhaps more importantly, he was ready to be absorbed by that detail, ready to put the hours and the thought in, and ambitious for the brewery's future.

There is nothing to suggest that Arthur had anything like that appetite for a career in the brewery, nor even any particular interest, although he must have had some, for his father to have made out the will as he did. Arthur seems to have been always more drawn to the promise of life in politics than attending to what was probably for the most part rather humdrum work in the brewery. Although the brothers were now owners and partners, they were not as removed from the daily grind as a modern company director might be. They wrote their own letters, paid bills and oversaw orders, and undertook numerous other most unglamorous tasks.

Benjamin Lee had relied on the steady hands of the Pursers, and Arthur and Edward were ready to follow suit. Edward had a deep fondness for John Tertius, obvious in the affectionate tone he used about him in an 1874 letter to Adelaide, by then his wife:

> Purser is all right although he upset his poney carriage outside the Park Gate on Saturday he had done <u>exactly</u> the same thing on the same spot about 3 weeks ago dear old Silly – he has not injured himself beyond bruising his hip & is unable to stand.

The brothers wrote a joint letter to him from Mayfair in June 1869 expressing their appreciation of his work, and the hope that, even though their father was now gone, he would continue to work with them. They offered him £2,000 a year, and closed the letter in a way that almost suggested they saw John Tertius, in a work context at least, *in loco parentis*:

> We feel that though we have lost the advice and assistance of a father, we may hope to retain that of his friend whose opinion and candid advice we shall always highly value.

In his reply, Purser showed how touched he was by the open warmth of the brothers' expression of what he meant to them. He can only have appreciated that they were also ready to offer him a significant bump in pay:

> I have felt it a duty and a privilege to be the slightest use to your revered father's sons – and if in any way I can aid in bearing a portion of the cares and responsibilities that now in our Lord's Good Providence devolve upon you it will afford me the most sincere pleasure.

Even with such a committed and experienced manager, it was always going to be a tall order for Arthur to combine the life and work of an MP in London with that of a brewery partner whose involvement in all the minutiae of daily work at the brewery was expected. However, this wasn't immediately tested, because as soon as the general election of November 1868 was over, returning Gladstone and his Liberal majority, Sir Arthur faced a challenge to the legitimacy of his win.

The challenge was successful, and he was unseated as a result. Members of his election team had extended promises of employment, and in some cases envelopes of cash, to those who agreed to vote for him. It is worth noting that the presiding judge, the deeply unpopular William Keogh, said in open court that he would have been far happier had he been able to rise from the bench having said that the petition had failed. Keogh wanted it recorded that Sir Arthur had not himself been guilty of corrupt transactions.

This was cold comfort to an angry and embarrassed Sir Arthur. The election was declared void in February 1869, and in early March it began to look as if one Guinness was just substitutable with another, for Sir Arthur's supporters wondered whether Edward Cecil would consider standing. Yes, he would indeed, and he published a circular in which he expressed great relish at the prospect. He was quick to define his political principles as 'those held by my father and brother', in that he was pro-Conservatism, and against the looming disestablishment of the Church of Ireland, and he stressed his commitment to his 'native City':

> I cannot but regard this Requisition as generous proof that the good-will and confidence often before shown to my family by the citizens of Dublin are unabated ...
>
> The fact that my business and prospects in life are altogether bound up with the prosperity of the trade in Dublin, I trust will be accepted as a guarantee that I will

devote my best energies to the protection and development of the mercantile interests of our City.

Sir Arthur was his brother and his partner, and it would take
more than the unseemly fallout of the last election for Edward
Cecil to distance himself from him. Edward Cecil's initial enthusiasm did not last, however, and he withdrew his candidacy before
the writ for the new election was issued in 1870.

In May of that year, Isaac Butt got in touch with Sir Arthur.
Butt was a capable and distinguished barrister, and later politician, who was perhaps then best known for defending the leader
of the Repeal Association, William Smith O'Brien, and a number
of other Young Irelanders in 1848. He had spent the four years
up to 1869 defending Fenian prisoners and in February 1870, as
president of the Amnesty Association, persuaded Gladstone to
agree to an amnesty for the Fenians, although what finally transpired was generally felt to be too little, too late. On 19 May of
that year he formed the Home Government Association (which
would become the Home Rule Party), and four days later, on 23
May, he wrote to Sir Arthur. He had, he said, been approached to
stand as a candidate himself, but he had declined.

If your brother proposes offering himself I will take
no part that will interfere with him. I would be glad
instead as far as I could to aid him ... A totally new
spirit has risen in the city of which you will soon see
general proof.

For my own part I am persuaded that the most
conservative measure that could be carried would be
the grant of an Irish parliament to manage Irish affairs
with the Imperial parliament still directing matters of
Imperial concern.

If you and your brother could see your way to join
in this he would be triumphantly returned and I would

then be free to use every exertion to have him put forward
and to secure his return <u>on very different terms from the
last contest</u>.

Butt's approach with the Home Rule movement, as expressed in
his letter, was essentially federalist, and acknowledged the role of
the empire. This kept the door open for those, largely Protestant,
Conservatives like the Guinnesses to espouse it. Many did, especially those who detested Gladstone for his tenant-friendly land
reforms. Not without a market did the Belleek pottery company
in Fermanagh produce a special edition chamber pot with
Gladstone's face inside, on the base.

The brothers were standing at a remarkable crossroads. The
Guinnesses might have thrown their lot in with Butt. Edward
Cecil could conceivably have stood as a Home Rule candidate
and been part of the wave of similar MPs returned in the 1874
general election. But the Guinness brothers held fast to the family's long-held belief that Ireland could flourish best as part of the
Union. The contemporary record of this comes not from Edward
Cecil himself but from Arthur. Butt had suggested that Arthur
discuss the matter both with Edward and with David Plunket. He
was William Plunket's brother and a Tory MP, who would in time
be best man at Arthur's wedding. Arthur did so, and wrote back
to Butt in the following terms:

[My brother] has resolved not to contest Dublin, but I
must say, as you have alluded to a rumour that there
was a chance of his adopting what are commonly called
National views and opinions, such was not the case, for
while none can feel more strongly a truly National desire
for the advancement of Ireland materially and intellectu-
ally, we do not and cannot think this is to be achieved by
Repeal or by any half measure of Repeal, but by the deter-
mination of the Irish nation to oblige their representatives

to enforce irrespective of party the rights of those they represent which they now almost entirely neglect.

There is something peculiar about this letter, which does not quite engage with Butt's 'half measure of Repeal'. It may be explained by the unusual circumstances, necessitated by Butt's approach to Arthur rather than Edward in the first instance, of Arthur's replying on Edward's behalf, while at the same time expressing what they together feel and think. In any event, the spelling out of their Unionism was a sidebar. Edward's decision not to stand in Dublin had been made before Butt's letter. In fact he would never now stand for election, though Arthur returned to the political fray in 1874, retaining his stance against Home Rule.

Gladstone, whose declared mission was 'to pacify Ireland', to use that quote which has inspired so many school examiners, did not achieve it. He did eventually bring forward two Home Rule bills, in 1886 and 1893, but both attempts failed, the first in the Commons and the second in the Lords. No part of Ireland was in any way pacified. Nationalists and Unionists alike had rejected the middle course, and the middle course itself had run aground.

In 1871 Arthur, now 30, married the 21-year-old Olivia (Olive) Hedges-White, one of six children of the Earl and Countess of Bantry. They were married in Bantry by the Bishop of Tuam, and then got into a carriage to be drawn by a crowd of people to the bride's home, Bantry House, for the wedding breakfast. It was February, but the parish church was filled with camellias, azaleas, dahlias and tiny seasonal lily of the valley.

Arthur also had a dazzling array of gifts for his bride: a diamond tiara, a diamond necklace, two pairs of diamond earrings and a diamond ring, as well as a dressing case with silver gilt fittings, monogrammed in raised pink coral. After the speeches and toasts, the newlyweds set off for Macroom Castle, the earl's seat which would pass to Olive. The bride changed out of her white satin wedding dress into violet velveteen with a matching bonnet, and the couple left for their wedding tour of the Holy Land.

The marriage certificate records the occupations of both Arthur and his father Benjamin Lee as 'Baronet', which of course was the truth, but not the whole truth. Simply being a baronet did not occupy father or son. But it indicates the ultimate value placed, in nineteenth-century society, on rank within the social hierarchy. Arthur entered St Anne's as his address on the marriage certificate, and he and Olive went to live there together, with Ashford Castle in Galway as their country home.

Arthur's political career faced a staggered start, and he focused his attention elsewhere for a while, until the next general election was called in 1874. He and Olive began a series of enormous building projects at St Anne's and Ashford. They commissioned more or less a full rebuild of St Anne's, and added the variety of elements to Ashford that explains its stylistic mix today. Olive loved gardens and embarked on a long programme of development in the grounds at both houses. She must have been delighted when she (and her head gardener) discovered a new rose, to be named 'Souvenir de St Anne's'.

Arthur also worked with Edward on bringing another Dublin Exhibition to fruition in 1872. Though it was nowhere near as brave or big an undertaking to get this new exhibition off the ground as it had been for Benjamin Lee in the 1860s, it was still a huge public event, closely watched and publicly analysed.

The Exhibition Palace had been conceived, of course, not just as the venue for the 1865 exhibition itself, but as a lasting venue for all kinds of intellectual and cultural events. The building had only attracted a few bookings since, in dribs and drabs, consisting of amusements generally regarded as of rather low grade. Finally the Guinnesses stepped in. A new exhibition seemed just the thing to make good use of it and to give it a boost. The *Freeman's Journal* wrote that it had been a 'gaunt pile, melancholy in its lonely grandeur, sarcastic and reproachful in its waste and uselessness', but now it was prepared for another exhibition.

Over a busy five months the building was transformed, and filled with exhibits of interest and beauty, ready for its spring opening. These preparations do not appear to have been an energising experience for Edward, who wrote on 10 May 1872 to his cousin Adelaide, whom he would marry the following year, 'I am half mad with this horrid Exhibition which thank goodness will now be opened in a few hours'.

To be a success the exhibition had to be accessible, and this was a real gripe of the *Freeman*. It ought to be cheap to make it properly popular, the newspaper asserted, adding 'cheapness is the one desideratum which the enterprise lacks'. Although this piece, published in June 1872, was dotted with respectful references to 'the generosity and magnificent public spirit of the Brothers Guinness, who so worthily maintain the honour of an honoured name', and to their quiet and modest acts, it also held the kernel of what was to be a running argument.

After the first two weeks, the entry fee was reduced to a shilling from half a crown, which of course brought a visit there more within the grasp of ordinary working families. As in 1865, the discounted shilling rate did not apply on a Saturday, but this now struck many as somewhat out of touch for the two young men who employed so many workers at the brewery, given that for most people the Saturday afternoon half-holiday represented their hours of leisure. People would have to lose wages by taking time off work. The *Freeman* really got into its stride:

the Exhibition must remain a closed building for every working man and his family. With a density which is astounding in gentlemen accustomed to serve the public, Saturday is set apart for high folk, high prices and hifalu-tin … But Saturday is the free day of the workman, and no idler should filch it from him.

The pricing structure was changed, with Saturdays becoming shilling-entry days, and the *Freeman* printed an acknowledgement of this, giving themselves credit for remonstrating 'with the Brothers Guinness and their representatives upon the policy which excluded every workman from the Palace and its enjoyment.' Arthur was fed up with the newspaper by this point and wrote a response taking issue with any suggestion that a policy of exclusion was at play. 'We very much regret to find Sir Arthur in a bad temper,' the *Freeman* announced gleefully, delighted to have provoked a response. Arthur had not yet found the balance between tolerating and parrying the thrusts of the press in mischievous form.

Unfortunately, 1872's exhibition was a feebler affair than 1865's, and only 400,000 visitors came. The brothers had created for the exhibition a guarantee against loss, and as a result of this Edward was left with the site and some of the buildings. He later made over part of this as a gift to University College Dublin, whose degrees were first awarded by the Royal University of Ireland, but which from 1908 became a constituent college of the new National University of Ireland.

The year after the exhibition saw the most significant change in Edward Cecil's life, which was his marriage to Adelaide Maria Guinness. Like his father, he married within the family. He and Adelaide shared great-great-grandparents in Richard Guinness and Elizabeth Read: their respective great-grandfathers were the brothers Arthur I, the brewery founder, and Samuel, the goldbeater at the sign of the Hand and Hammer. Adelaide Guinness had grown up in Dublin, where her family home was by the sea at Deepwell in Blackrock, about four miles south of St Stephen's Green.

Her father was a barrister and MP, but he died when she was only 13. He left the family with no money, and Adelaide described her childhood, and that of her sisters Mildred, Geraldine and Edith, as lived in 'grinding poverty'. It is a phrase not usually associated with a seaside mansion, a team of servants and trips to Paris, where her mother had family connections and an apartment full of dogs. Her mother was not thrilled at the idea of Adelaide being married, appalled that there would now be 'nobody to exercise the dogs', but she doesn't appear to have made any attempt to prevent the marriage, and it went ahead in Ascot, west of London.

Before the ceremony Adelaide went to stay with her sister Geraldine and her brother-in-law the Rev. Beauchamp Kerr-Pearce. He was Rector of Ascot and performed the wedding ceremony on 20 May 1873. In December 1870 Edward had bought the lease of a London flat at 5 Berkeley Square, very close to his father's house in Norfolk Street, and so it was there that the couple stayed as newlyweds, walking in the gardens as a gentle winding down after the busy wedding day. Adelaide recorded it very simply in her diary:

> May 20. Tuesday. Married Edward at Ascot. Both behaved very well. Lovely day and very pretty wedding. Went to Berkeley Sq. Had a walk late in Park – was very tired.

Their wedding did not draw the same attention from the newspapers as had that of Arthur and Olive. Edward was a partner in the brewery, and as the son of a rich businessman was an eligible bachelor if it was money you were after. But he was still young at 25, and though the 1872 exhibition had raised his profile he had yet to make his mark in any significant way. Arthur, as the eldest, the baronet, and already elected to a seat in parliament (albeit swiftly unseated), was, for the moment, the brother more in the public eye.

Olive was a beautiful young aristocrat, which also accorded a measure of instant celebrity. When Arthur married her, periodicals from the *Cork Examiner* to the *Queen* reported the details of their movements, their clothes, their jewels and their notable guests, in a kind of scrutiny new to Arthur and Edward, who would both have to become accustomed to it for the rest of their lives.

Edward and Adelaide – Ned and Dodo to one another – began their six-week honeymoon with a week in Paris, which gave Adelaide the opportunity of airing her perfect French for her new husband. There they spent time with Adelaide's French family and connections, before leaving to travel around Germany by train and steamer, then on to Austria and Italy. From Lake Maggiore they crossed the Alps in a carriage, pulled over the Simplon Pass by a team of six horses. They lunched at Simplon and that evening dined in Switzerland, moving on quickly to Geneva, and Chamonix, then back via Paris, where they dined with a Montebello cousin, to Berkeley Square and the last night at the opera *L'Étoile du Nord*. Finally they returned to Dublin and St Stephen's Green, where Adelaide was happy to be making her new home:

> The house looking lovely. So very glad to be here again. Busy all day getting unpacked and settled. Went late for a drive with Neddy in the coach.

These whirling weeks of travel, opera, a luxurious apartment here, a mansion there, dinner in good company and quiet moments for two were not out of kilter with the Guinnesses' married life to come. Ned bought another house, Farmleigh, in the Phoenix Park, intended as a country bolthole – yet still close enough to be practical for attendance at St James's Gate, for Ned had no intention of letting the pleasures of travel, an active social circle and married life divert him from brewery matters for too long. He and Adelaide stayed at Farmleigh for the first time the October after they were married. The Park, full of oak, ash and beech trees, blazed with autumn colours as they walked through it together each day for Ned to cross the Liffey to work, and Adelaide to turn east for a day in town. Sometimes she drove her phaeton, a little open carriage, already old-fashioned even then, to meet him on his way home.

It was a happy time, precious to both. Both Ned's parents had died before he was 21, and though Adelaide's mother was still alive there seems to have been a certain amount of coolness in her relationship with her daughter. Adelaide had also lost her father very early, and even as a child had suffered anxieties about money. Together, now, she and Ned had an opportunity to create a secure and loving new family life of their own, buoyed up by plenty of money and property, and by Ned's staunch dedication to the prosperity of the brewery. By the time of that first week at Farmleigh Adelaide must already have suspected that she was pregnant, as five months later she noted efficiently: '29th March. Sunday morning. Baby born at ¼ to 6. Boy.' This was my great-grandfather Rupert.

They had gone to London for the birth, as had become the fashion, and for Adelaide it meant being near her sister at Ascot, and her mother, now living in Brighton. The primary relationship of warmth and support was with her sister, nicknamed Gee. Ned stayed with his wife and their new son, Rupert Edward Cecil Lee, at Berkeley Square for a few weeks, and at the end of April 1874 they all moved, with the nurse and servants and the complicated additional baggage the baby necessitated, to a hotel at Virginia Water at the edge of Windsor Great Park. From here they brought Rupert to be baptised in the church where they had been married, and by June were home again to Farmleigh and St Stephen's Green.

Farmleigh was another house to renovate, decorate and fill with lovely things, and it was about this time that Ned began what would become a serious art collection. His first major acquisition, in 1874, was Rembrandt's 1629 painting *Judas Returning the Thirty Pieces of Silver*, which appropriately enough is widely recognised as the artist's first masterpiece, painted when he was 23. Ned too was still a young man, at 27, when he bought it, with plenty of time to develop his eye for art, and to make sufficient money to fund his collection.

Dublin high society, into which Benjamin Lee had led his family, pivoted around the Lord Lieutenant, his wife the Vicereine, and the Viceregal court. The Lord Lieutenant was the British monarch's personal representative in Ireland and the head of the Irish administration at Dublin Castle, aided by the Lord Chancellor and the two most senior civil servants: the Chief Secretary and the Under-Secretary. The administration's function was largely the implementation of decisions taken in London, and the body of civil servants grew until, by the end of the nineteenth century, more than 3,000 people were employed in central and local government.

The Lord Lieutenant's job in restless Ireland was not a popular one, despite the attractions of the beautiful Viceregal Lodge in the Phoenix Park, which had been built in the mid-eighteenth century, and had not long afterwards been bought as the official residence, for the monarch needed somewhere suitable to stay in Dublin, and the Lord Lieutenant needed somewhere suitably opulent to host balls. Lords Lieutenant tended not to stay for more than a couple of years. Very occasionally one might come back for a second tour. James Hamilton, the Duke of Abercorn, who arrived in 1874, was one of those rare birds, serving from 1866 to 1868 under Derby and then Disraeli, but resigning after Gladstone's general election victory. When the Tories won again in 1874, he returned to the Viceregal Lodge as the Guinnesses' neighbour.

Although Farmleigh and the Viceregal Lodge (today Áras an Uachtaráin, the official residence of the President of Ireland) are both situated in the Phoenix Park, it is no ordinary park, at 1,750 acres, and there is plenty of green space between the two houses, which lie about a mile and a half apart. Farmleigh lies about the same distance from the Chief Secretary's Lodge (now Deerfield, the official residence of the United States Ambassador to Ireland) which was also within the Park. The Guinnesses moved into the Park in the same year that the All-Ireland Polo Club made its home there on the Nine Acres. The members of the Phoenix Cricket Club, founded by John Parnell, father of Charles Stewart Parnell, had already been playing there for nearly 30 years.

When parties and balls were given at the Viceregal Lodge, the names of the guests, and often the selection of music played, were reported in the newspapers. The guest lists were given in two categories: the titled, usually in order of precedence, and then the commoners, usually in alphabetical order. This meant that Lord and Lady Plunket and Sir Arthur and Lady Olivia Guinness appeared in one category, while plain Mr and Mrs Edward Guinness appeared in another. But appear they did, not only at dinners and parties at the lodge, but at other events at which the Viceroy was present, including art exhibitions, concerts, receptions and society weddings.

During Castle Season, which kicked off in January each year, everything moved into town, and at the Viceroy's suite at Dublin Castle there was another round of balls, dinner parties and levées, and the presentation of debutantes, after the fashion of St James's. The biggest event of the Castle Season was the St Patrick's Day Ball in March. There, as Frances Gerard documented in *Picturesque Dublin*, the dancing was so athletic that once a uniformed general was tripped up by an over-enthusiastic youngster. He was stretchered off, and 'it was found that the gallant officer, having escaped the Russian guns, had broken his leg on the polished floor of St Patrick's Hall'.

After the Castle Season there was steeplechasing at Punchestown Racecourse in county Kildare, and the Guinnesses liked to have a house party at no. 80, which included two days of racing. Ned would send on ahead a packed lunch to be properly laid out on tables at the racecourse, and of course it was a delicious one, exquisitely prepared. Ned's private secretary recorded in 1883:

> For the two days lunch for 18 people. I gave out: 36 champagne, 6 sherry, 12 light claret, 2 curacoa. All was drunk except 4 bottles of champagne. 5 of Waterhouses knives and one of our own metal goblets were lost on the course, also Arthur's hat.

Sometimes the Guinnesses drove to Punchestown, with Ned at the reins, something he loved. Another family story recounts how, the very first time his father allowed Ned to drive a coach, he drove the horses hard and fast through the entrance to the brewery yard, and narrowly escaped a collision with a cask of beer that happened to be rolling across the yard at the same time. It was a close shave, but did not put him off driving horses at speed: driving, especially a four-in-hand, was a lifelong passion.

It is amusing to realise that even a son as aligned with his father's interests, temperament and ambition as Ned could still, as a teenager, provide a few hairy moments for 'the Governor' – which is also, quite probably, why it was a story his siblings told. By the 1880s Ned and Adelaide had stopped driving to Punchestown and would travel there on the Viceregal train instead, with a whole carriage reserved for their party of 16 to 20 people. A family story tells that a witty railway porter once chalked on the Viceroy's private compartments 'His X', and on Ned's 'His XX', in reference to the Guinness Extra Stout label.

From the early days of their marriage, Ned and Adelaide loved to entertain, something that distinguished their approach to life from Benjamin Lee's, with his wholesome régime of early suppers and family prayers. The Guinnesses approached the social scene with the supreme confidence of a couple who were young, beautiful, rich and fun, and who knew their city inside out, and could conquer it on a whim. Within a few years the

St Stephen's Green balls were rivalling those of the Viceroy (by this time Lord Cowper), not just in the magnificence of their setting but also in people's desperation for invitations.

The society columns picked over the details of decorations, food, drink, music, guests and clothes with undiminished appetite. The newspapers were not shy about discussing the costs; the *Irish Times* noted breathlessly in the summer of 1879 that Lady Olive Guinness had spent £4,000 on a ball, opting for 'the choicest and costliest blooms and blossoms'. Nor were they above fanning the flames of the rivalry between Olive and Adelaide. Olive had achieved 'the success of the season, though it is shared with her sister-in-law, Mrs Guinness, who had an equally brilliant reception a few nights before'.

In 1881 the fashionable set couldn't sleep a wink for worrying about whether or not they would receive invitations to 'Mrs Guinness's ball'. That year she not only opened the Dublin Season on 1 February with a ball at no. 80, but nine days later she also held a Grand Fancy Ball. At this, no one wearing current uniform or court dress would be permitted entry. Several newspapers, including the *Dublin Daily Telegraph*, regarded this as a patriotic act and a stimulus to trade, because of the flood of orders that would flow from Mrs Guinness's thousand guests to the milliners and tailors of Ireland.

Ned had two outfits on the go, first an old Florentine costume and later a Cavalier, while Adelaide was resplendent as Madame de Pompadour. The guests and their dressmakers rose to the occasion. Lord Cowper, the Viceroy, came as Cesare Borgia, and others represented Mary Queen of Scots, Henry IV, Aida, Marguerite de Valois and White Dresden China. Everyone played the game, though not all opted for glamour: Lady Drogheda went as Old Mother Hubbard.

Life now largely followed a prescribed pattern over the year. This meant Dublin over the winter, until Punchestown, then Farmleigh over Easter, and London for the season, which after 1877 no longer meant Berkeley Square, but 5 Grosvenor Place, leased from the Duke of Westminster. After Cowes for the sailing, and Scotland for shooting, it was home again to Ireland for another winter.

But life was not all champagne hangovers, legs breaking mid-dance, hats lost to a gusty steeplechase, hothouse flowers scenting every intake of breath and general glittering. There was more to it.

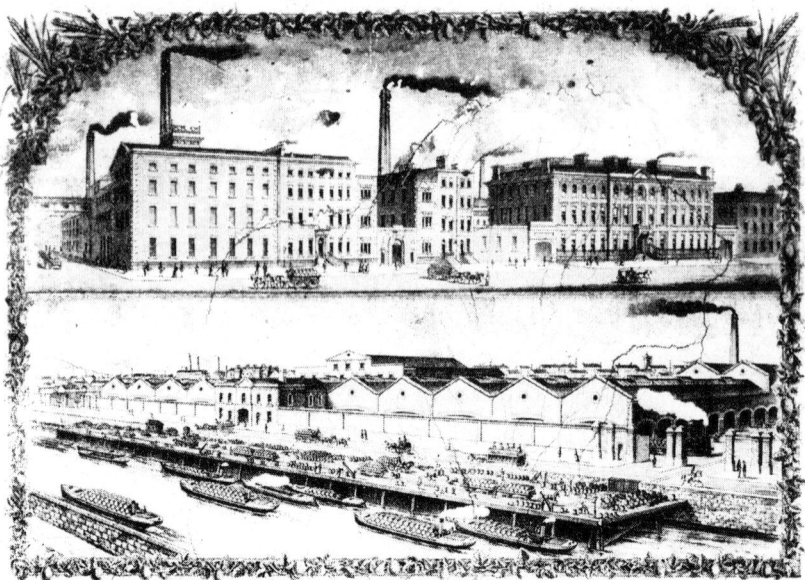

Illustration from an advertising showcard for
Guinness's St James's Gate Porter Brewery, *c*.1890.

NINE

BY MUTUAL CONSENT

For Ned in particular, this meant St James's Gate. In 1873, the acquisition of a site on the far side of James's Street, stretching all the way down the hill to the river, meant that the footprint of the brewery doubled. The increase in size, and the logistical difficulties this brought, triggered one of the brewery's most remarkable innovations. A narrow-gauge railway was designed and constructed on the brewery premises, to carry raw materials from the hop and malt stores to the brewing rooms, full casks down to the river ready for loading, empty casks to the washing sheds and waste materials for disposal.

The railway was designed and built by Samuel Geoghegan, an engineer who was also a member of the Purser family: his mother was the daughter of John Purser Junior and the sister of John Tertius Purser. Samuel's brother, William Purser Geoghegan, was now head brewer at St James's Gate. In 1869, after completing an apprenticeship with a firm in Birmingham, Samuel had gone to Smyrna (now İzmir, in Turkey) to work with the Ottoman Railway for two years.

In 1871 he moved to India, where he was first assistant and then executive engineer working on the construction of a two-mile-long bridge over the river Chenab in Punjab, and afterwards district locomotive superintendent working on the railway near Delhi. He came home in 1874 and was appointed chief engineer at the Guinness brewery. He had all the skills needed to figure out the railway, down to solving the thorniest problems, such as how to get the railway to cross between two sites with a 50-foot difference in levels. His solution to that one was to build a steep spiral tunnel and pass the line under James's Street to connect the two parts of the brewery site.

Although the first public railway had been laid in Ireland, from Dublin to what was then Kingstown 40 years earlier, in 1834, what Geoghegan built was the largest private railway in the country. It ran to a full eight miles; later, a short broad-gauge line was laid from the lower site beside the river, to connect the brewery infrastructure to the rail terminal at Kingsbridge. This was Irish engineering, with ironwork done by a local foundry on nearby Cork Street, but it is worth noting how much of Geoghegan's knowledge and experience had been gained working in imperial India, an example of knowledge transfer from one colonised country to another.

As we will see later, the search for new knowledge and the ready adoption of new technology were two of Ned's many trademarks. An interest in transport developments had always been an essential aspect of running the brewery. We know, for example, from their careful records of personal expenditure, that Arthur II had invested in the Liverpool and Manchester Railway in 1830, and Benjamin Lee had invested in the Great Western Railway in 1852.

The brewery had been producing 236,000 hogsheads of beer a year when Ned and Arthur inherited it in 1868. Eight years later, in 1876, this had shot up to 525,000. The profits were shooting up, too. The year the brothers inherited, there were profits of £102,000, and by 1876 they were up to £302,000. This trend was set to continue, and by 1880 the brewery at St James's Gate would be the largest in the world.

Despite these modernising changes and the seemingly unstoppable growth in the popularity of Guinness, Arthur took far less of an interest in the brewery than Ned did. There are also hints in Ned's private correspondence that relations between the brothers were coming under tension. Writing to Adelaide in April 1873 about a social event, he remarked that the Plunkets would not be able to attend, '& I sincerely hope Arthur & Olive will not either t'would be much pleasanter if they did not'. A week later he called on his sister-in-law, who 'was very civil & friendly & it is so pleasant they both funk saying anything nasty before me.' It cannot have been easy to work together when the personal relationship was strained. As well as Arthur's lack of interest in brewing matters, he also had preoccupations elsewhere, such as having to focus on his new election campaign in 1874.

First, though, Arthur had to deal with an unpleasant libel case which stemmed from another dust-up with the *Freeman's Journal*. Under the heading 'Reported Social Scandal' it published a report, on the same page as an editorial about the evils of divorce, about a figure from 'our "upper ten"' (a New York phrase of the time more or less equivalent to our usage of 'the one per cent') forced to leave the country to 'seek refuge from a charge of a bigamous nature', while his wife 'quitted his protection a few days since and has rejoined her family'.

The latter phrasing was the typically euphemistic way of describing a separation, but there was nothing euphemistic about referring to a charge of a bigamous nature. Arthur was furious, and issued proceedings against Sir John Gray, the newspaper owner, who had also been MP for Kilkenny for nearly ten years. The family solicitor, Fred Sutton, briefed two silks, one of whom, Francis McDonagh QC, argued in the strongest terms that Arthur, though not named, was clearly identified in the piece, and that what was written about the bigamous charge, and his wife having left him, was 'a libel of the blackest dye'.

Arthur appeared in court to give evidence that he and Olive had been in London together, and that he had read the article himself and had also heard of it through gossip in the Carlton Club and the lobby of the House of Commons. Did he read it again after hearing this chatter?

> Well, I had read it several times before. I got enough of
> it ... Upon my oath, there is not the slightest shadow

of foundation that I had reason to apprehend a bigamous charge, or anything connected with it.

Nor, he stated, had Olive ever left him. Counsel for Sir John Gray now said that Gray wanted to issue an apology: he had been away when it had happened, and nothing would be more foreign to his feeling than to cast the slightest blemish on the fair fame and reputation of a character so unsullied as that of Sir Arthur Guinness. Olive's father, the Earl of Bantry, was in court too, and in a private consultation he and Arthur agreed that this apology so late in the day was insufficient, whereupon a round of applause broke out in court.

However, when the case was returned for trial, Arthur, through McDonagh, said that he had never injured a citizen of Dublin and did not mean to commence now. He wanted to see Sir John Gray unconditionally liberated and without further apology or public atonement, from the prosecution. A crowd roared its approval as Arthur came out of court.

Sir John Gray was as much a businessman as the Guinness brothers were. He had bought the *Freeman* in 1841, and had taken the opportunity of the lifting of duties imposed on advertising, and later on newspapers themselves, to increase the circulation of the paper from about 3,000 per day to about 10,000 by the time of Arthur's libel case. Of course the higher the circulation, and the more people reading a libellous piece, the higher the potential damages.

Gray's son Edmund Dwyer Gray would succeed his father as proprietor and triple circulation again, to 30,000, before floating the company in 1887. The newspaper's life cycle of expansion, succession, greatly increased profits and public flotation would be similar to the brewery's. Arthur had always understood the power of the press, and he watched it increase, along with literacy levels, as the twentieth century appeared on the horizon. When the opportunity later arose in 1900 he bought two of the

Freeman's rivals, the Unionist-leaning *Dublin Daily Express* and *Dublin Evening Mail.*

When the general election arrived in 1874, this time everything went Arthur's way. If it hadn't, his focus might have been pulled back towards the brewery, his energy directed to developing plans for its future, and, importantly, figuring out how he and Ned could work in concert. But the electorate spoke, and for him politics prevailed. He was returned for the City of Dublin, Gladstone's government was displaced and Benjamin Disraeli formed a new Tory government in its place; Arthur spent the next six years attending the House of Commons.

His contributions were unremarkable. He raised the question of an Industrial and Fine Arts Museum in Dublin, and talked about the necessity for members of the Dublin Stock Exchange to have direct telegraphic communication similar to that enjoyed by the members of the stock exchanges of Edinburgh, Liverpool, Manchester and Glasgow. And there were local issues like drainage in Dublin, or the Lough Corrib Navigation Bill, though the latter was local to Arthur in Ashford, rather than to his Dublin City constituency.

Arthur was also overseeing the creation of a fine statue of Benjamin Lee at St Patrick's Cathedral, made in bronze by John Henry Foley and paid for out of public subscriptions. He was concerned that the statue might need to be on a higher pedestal, and had even gone so far as to have a temporary pedestal made. The sculptor replied politely but firmly: 'I purposely designed the pedestal so as to allow the figures to be seen as little foreshortened as possible for if a sitting statue be placed high, in the front or principle [sic] view it loses much of its proper effect.' He suggested that the temporary pedestal could easily be tried out, but clearly had no intention of taking artistic direction from the client.

The statue was erected in the grounds of the cathedral in 1875, and formally handed over to the Dean and Chapter in December 1876, although sadly by this time Foley had died.

The statue was well received. The *Illustrated London News* noticed 'the thoughtfulness of the attitude and the benevolence of expression in the fine head', and it was mentioned in many of the appreciations of Foley published on his death, usually as being one of Foley's top three works, the other two being Prince Albert depicted as Chancellor of the University of Cambridge, and General Stonewall Jackson. Today, the ashes of my brother Rory's wife, Mira Guinness, lie at the base of the statue of Benjamin Lee, and a Guinness family rose grows there.

And so, with the development of Ashford, managing estate matters, travelling between Ireland and England, keeping the newspapers honest, learning how to be an MP and memorialising his father, Arthur had plenty to attend to and could be forgiven, even in this family of obsessive multi-taskers, for not being in as constant attendance at the brewery as Ned was. Absorption in the brewery for Ned was obviously not fuelled by financial necessity, but nor was it necessarily a choice, given how close he had been to his father, and how deeply he must have felt the old man's desire for the family to hang on to the reins.

Carrying the expectations of earlier generations can be a dragging weight on the shoulders. In any event, in the three years after Ned's marriage in 1873, he mulled over what the future might look like. The brothers could continue in a partnership, which would, it was already clear, mean more work for Ned, and shared profits, but also the relief of shared responsibility. Another option was for Ned to ask Arthur to buy him out, and retire before he turned 30 in 1877. Or, a third option, he could suggest that he buy Arthur out, and carry on alone.

The difficulties of an unequal partnership are self-evident, and Ned knew that he wouldn't be able to force Arthur to be interested, even if he were able to force him to attend the brewery more often. A presence compelled is worth half that which is voluntary. It is quite possible that both their wives, with whatever frisson of competition shivered between them, each with a deep knowledge and understanding of her own husband, did not relish the idea of the two brothers being bound together at work.

It has often been suggested that Arthur's wife Olive was ready for her husband to distance himself from the brewery for the snobbish reason that there was something distasteful about brewing, or indeed anything related to manufacture or commerce. This may have been the case, with Olive the product of an upbringing in an aristocratic family, but even if it is true it does not describe in the round either Olive's character or her view of people, as her later life of philanthropy and war work illustrated.

The brothers were no longer tightly roped by Benjamin Lee's will. At Ned's request they had created a new deed of partnership which lightened the penalties for leaving the brewery as initially envisaged by their father's will: the retiring partner would now walk away with half the brewery's value (calculated on the goodwill of the business, plus the plant) and half of the current year's profit. But probably there was something in Ned which made him determined not to be one to withdraw, when he had already given more than ten years of his life to the brewery, knew it inside out, and knew what more it had to give. The third option began to seem the most plausible, and so Ned began the process of negotiating his way to sole control.

As early as March 1875 Arthur had indicated clearly that retirement from the partnership was what he wanted, but he flip-flopped on his decision. Later that year, in November, Ned wrote to Arthur from Berkeley Square:

> I may as well say a word referring to our conversation last March when you expressed a wish to retire and named five hundred thousand pounds as matters stood on the 31st December, 1874 as the sum that would enable you to do so. A few days afterwards I told you that as you wished it I would accept your own terms. Since then we

had a talk on the subject in London and I gathered you had rather changed your mind about it.

Ned said one of his strongest motives in offering 'to take on my shoulders a double risk was not to let things at James's Gate stand in the way of a Peerage for you'. His concern about the peerage – at that time still only putative – was that

> at a future day when the Peerage might actually be under offer it might happen to be the very time I may be intent myself of getting out of it and therefore unable to release you and I was willing to undertake as a younger man that which any later in my life I would probably never dream of as I have no wish to spend more of the best years of my life than I can help at such anxious work.

Arthur's expectation of a peerage could only have rested on his service as an MP. Even that record seemed too slight to some. When a whisper that it was about to happen reached the press in the autumn of 1879, it was reported in the following bemused terms in the *York Herald*:

> For the second time it is rumoured that Sir Arthur Guinness is to be raised to the peerage. Why, or wherefore, nobody seems to know. Probably the rumour has no foundation, in fact.

Back in 1874 a peerage for Arthur had been an even less substantial idea, but one that grabbed the attention of the brothers, who turned the idea over and over, together and separately, dreaming about who might do what, and when. There is the sense, in that letter from Ned, that he knew the peerage was something his brother longed for, that if it came it would immediately claim priority and trump other concerns. Ned understood and

accepted this. He wanted Arthur to know how his mind had
been working:

> I would not have written all this but that as we shall not
> be able unfortunately to meet for so long I like to tell
> you what I have been for a long time wishing to have an
> opportunity to say to you.

Both brothers must have been hugely helped by the openness
between them. Neither saw a future in which the brewery played
the most significant part of his life. Each admitted to wanting an
exit strategy. In May 1876 they had reached a phase of making
temporary extensions to their partnership agreement while a new
one was negotiated. Ned was keen not to let things drift, writing
to both Arthur and their solicitor, Fred Sutton. He could not
feel justified, he wrote to Arthur, in leaving things as they stood,
and could not renew the deed as it was. He was conscious of the
money that could be lost to his heirs were he to die unexpectedly without the changes having been made. He used an identical
expression in both letters, having 'one child to provide for &
probably more coming'.

In another of those poignant echoes through time, this turn
of phrase recalls the 1790 expression of the first Arthur: 'one &
twenty born to us, & more likely yet to come'. He told Sutton
that he would have to amend his will 'until I can get Arthur's
time and attention to sign a new deed'. The current deed's
expiry date in June did drift past, despite further letters, and
eventually the two men agreed and signed on a new deed. But
by autumn they had struck an agreement that Ned would buy
Arthur out. This accord, signed by both on 12 October 1876,
gave even more favourable terms to the retiring partner than the
recently agreed deed had.

Arthur was to receive £600,000 (rather than the £400,000
he would have been entitled to under the new deed of

partnership) for his share of the goodwill and plant. On top of this was a half-share in the year's profit, £80,000. The total of £680,000 was to be paid in six instalments over four years, to be completed by 1 August 1880. An unusually large withdrawal by Ned from the brewery in 1880, of £159,000, suggests that he might have taken this sum in order to complete his schedule of payments to Arthur.

The dissolution of the partnership was announced by a notice in the *Dublin Gazette* in December, to the effect that the partnership was 'this day dissolved by mutual consent', and that Ned would carry on alone 'under the name, style, and firm of "Arthur Guinness, Son and Co."'

Arthur was free, and rich, and could hope that no whiff of beer would linger, to hold back the peerage he so desperately hoped was waiting in the wings. It would linger in the public imagination, though, long after he had finally walked away. He would forever be a brewer. James Joyce's *Ulysses*, published in 1922 when Arthur was already dead, was set in 1904, and mentions the brothers several times. Arthur appears as the brewer Lord Ardilaun, although he left the brewery while still plain Sir Arthur, and Ned as Lord Iveagh. A well-known passage describes the ennobled brothers, their titles prefixed with the brewer's bung (the name for the stopper in a barrel), presiding over the brewing process of

> the foaming ebon ale which the noble twin brothers Bungiveagh and Bungardilaun brew ever in their divine alevats, cunning as the sons of deathless Leda. For they garner the succulent berries of the hop and mass and sift and bruise and brew them and they mix therewith sour juices and bring the must to the sacred fire and cease not night or day from their toil, those cunning brothers, lords of the vat.

Later, amid some rapid-fire drunk-talk, there's a glancing reference to the rhythms of a bar order: 'Two Ardilauns. Same here.' It is an amusing glimpse of what might have been, had Arthur not left when he did. And while surviving Purser family members, those brewing perfectionists, might have had some trenchant words to say about that 'ale', the lords of the vat have always been more than capable of being amused: there is a first edition of *Ulysses* in the Benjamin Iveagh Library at Farmleigh.

Arthur may have been able to put brewery duties out of his mind, but there were plenty more anxieties to flow into the space vacated. High on the list were tensions between tenants and landlords across the country. These had been simmering for years. They had been in no way cooled by Gladstone's Land Act of 1870, and issues of land ownership and tenant rights – encapsulated in the Land League's 'three Fs', fair rent, freedom of sale and fixity of tenure – were thrown into an even starker relief when the potato crop started showing blight, causing not only hardship in the moment, but the terror that the trauma of the Hungry Forties was about to revisit.

By 1879 agrarian disturbance and violence were breaking out all over the country. Isaac Butt was dead, and Charles Stewart Parnell had moved to the fore of the Home Rule movement. Rural Ireland was politicised, and Unionist Protestant landlords were generally regarded as the problem. The conditions inflicted on tenants as a class were so universally oppressive that no individual landlord's reasonable treatment of tenants really mattered, and it was more difficult than ever for those with any kind of dual allegiance to justify their position. Arthur was regarded, and regarded himself, as a good landlord, but his convinced Unionism and his open desire to live as a member of the landed gentry positioned him as the enemy.

In the summer of 1879 Arthur's agent at Ashford, William Burke, had a bucket of boiling water thrown over him as he rode through Cong. Although Arthur announced to his own tenants that he would offer rent abatements of 30 per cent and 20 per cent, there were notices plastered up promising violence against tenants who paid even reduced rents, and initially this infuriated him. Nothing, he told his tenants in early December,

> shall ever induce me to yield even one inch to such unworthy and disgraceful efforts to influence you and me, and create between us feelings of irritation and distrust which have never hitherto existed.

In the bizarre juxtaposition of worlds and experiences that the landlord-and-tenant system enshrined, Arthur had an exceptionally good woodcock-shooting party that same month. 'Sir Arthur Guinness and his parties have had large bags at Ashford, where there is generally the best sport in the country,' reported the *Truth*. But the disconnect did not last. Arthur had not realised what was actually happening to his tenants, but soon he saw their distress for himself.

On Christmas Eve 1879, weeks after denouncing the agitation, he came to Dublin and spoke at a hastily convened meeting at the Mansion House:

> every subscription and amount, however large, which can be obtained will be very inadequate to meet the necessities of the case. There are hundreds – for all I know, there may be thousands – but I can speak of my own district, where there are hundreds of families whose supply of potatoes has been very nearly consumed. Their credit is at an end, and what is to happen to these people unless the hand of charity comes in, save starvation, I do not know.

He proposed a resolution to set up a Dublin Mansion House Relief Fund. It was passed, and he contributed the first £200, with other contributions bringing it up almost immediately to £1,500. He delivered the same message to other meetings, including one at Ennis which brought landlords and tenants together, and pressed for rent reductions and long-term loans for improvements.

Against this background Arthur fought another general election in 1880, and he and commentators generally assumed that he would retain his Conservative seat and the other sitting MP, Maurice Brooks, would retain his for the Liberals. He spoke in defence of the landlord class and in repudiation of Home Rule, but could not, for obvious reasons, row in with the temperance movement. Its activists wanted a commitment to Sunday closing. Arthur would only go so far as to support shorter opening hours, and before he knew it the Conservative party had selected a second candidate, James Stirling, an enthusiastic temperance man who was happy to get behind not just Sunday closing but Saturday night closing. The Conservative strategy did not pay off. The count, in the Exhibition Palace, went on into the early hours, and when the result was declared it was a double victory for the Liberals, with both Maurice Brooks and Robert Lyons returned.

That was the end of Arthur in the House of Commons, and now the House of Lords beckoned. In April 1880 Disraeli finally offered him the peerage he had wanted for so long. Arthur was to be made a baron, and the name he chose was Ardilaun, after an island on his estate. The meaning of the original Irish ard oileán, or 'high island', harked back, whether by accident or design, to Oughterard, the 'high place' above Ardclough where the first Arthur Guinness and other family members were buried.

So it was as Lord Ardilaun that Arthur made perhaps his best-loved contribution to Dublin and Dubliners. He and Olive, now Lady Ardilaun, had a house on the east side of St Stephen's Green (Ned and Adelaide's great townhouse was on the south side of the Green). Several years previously he had entered into

discussions with other St Stephen's Green householders about
the future of the Green itself. It had deteriorated, as one newspaper put it, into a 'comparatively uninviting waste', and with
one of those sweeping, transformative gestures which his deep
pockets made possible, Arthur funded its purchase for the city,
investing £20,000 in transforming it through hard landscaping,
walks and seats, a man-made lake with a little island, foun-
tains and a gorgeous planting scheme of trees, shrubbery, grass
and flowers. The whole area was surrounded by a gravel ride
and enclosed with iron railings. With no particular ceremony
the gates were thrown open to the public at the end of July
1880, and it passed into the ownership of the city. It was a gift
to everyone, but most particularly to those without access to
gardens of their own.

The *Irish Times* was falling over itself with pleasure:

> To the poor of the neighbourhood, to the invalid,
> and to children who would too frequently otherwise
> be wheeled in perambulators or have wearily to walk
> through the dusty, hot, noisy streets during the summer
> time, the liberality of Lord Ardilaun will have offered a
> quiet and pleasant retreat ... there, too in summer and
> autumn evenings the large crowds who seek the cool
> breeze after the heat of the day will have in St Stephen's
> Green charming promenades ... instead of, as at present,
> thronging the streets ... Should the charm of music be
> at any time added to the many attractions of the place,
> either in consequence of the action of the residents of
> the square or otherwise, it would be difficult to conceive
> what else would be wanting to render the Green the
> ideal of a perfect resort for public enjoyment.

Even Arthur's old sparring partner, the *Freeman's Journal*, had to
hand it to him, and did so graciously:

We differ from Lord Ardilaun on most public questions, and have never hesitated to express that difference in decided language. We feel it, therefore, all the more incumbent upon us, as public journalists, to give expression to the warm feeling of gratitude which pervades all sections of the people of Dublin with reference to the princely gift which he has bestowed upon them. The value of such a Park as that which was yesterday opened can, both from a sanitary and a moral aspect, be scarcely over-estimated. It is a boon to the wealthy classes, but it is a priceless gift to their poorer neighbours. No man could yesterday walk through the Green and see the hundreds of little children playing about, with a look of unaccustomed pleasure in their poor, pale, pinched little faces, without feeling his heart touched, or without realising how much the poor will benefit by having such a place of healthy, harmless recreation in their midst.

The newspaper mentioned his 'characteristic modesty', his 'noble generosity' and 'a public spirit which was hereditary', and said it would be first in the queue to contribute to some sort of public testimony to him. In time this came about, in the form of a bronze statue in the park, paid for by public subscription. Like the figure of Benjamin Lee outside St Patrick's, Lord Ardilaun's figure is seated. The inscription notes that, by his generosity, 'this park was laid out and beautified for the use and enjoyment of the citizens of Dublin'.

At home in Ashford, nothing had settled down. Just up the road from Ashford Castle lived Captain Charles Boycott, a Norfolk-born agent notorious for his poor treatment of the tenants on Lord Erne's neighbouring Lough Mask estates. With 18 evictions looming in September 1880, the tenants took a stand. They refused the ejectment processes, and wrote to the absentee Lord Erne, with whom they had much more cordial relations, insisting that they would never again work for or have any communication with the hated Captain Boycott.

In a move that added a new word to the English language, local traders refused to supply Boycott with goods or services. He couldn't get a horse shod or food in. Anyone who did trade with, or agreed to work for Boycott was ostracised in turn. His blacksmith was threatened with murder; his laundress ordered to give up doing his washing; the telegraph messenger was blocked on his way from the post office. Boycott could get no workman to do anything. The tenants declared that they would 'hunt him out of the country'. By the end of October Lord Erne had to arrange for a team to come down from Ulster to gather the crops.

That October, while Boycott couldn't leave his house without being surrounded by a mob, William Burke, Arthur's agent, received an anonymous letter, reading:

> I see that Sir Arthur Guinness is about leaving Ireland for England. Its near time he did but he will never return, as there is a 'six-chambered' ready for him, for his tyrannical conduct to his mountain tenants. We dont forget him or you either at home or abroad there is another on the way for you, so look out for you ought to hear it 20 years ago.
>
> Tell your gaffer – Lord Ardilaun better known as 'Arthur' – that he had better look out for a corner in Monkstown along with his colleagues in tyranny, Leitrim, Mountmorres. There is more than one on the lookout.
>
> An Avenger

Lord Leitrim had been killed in 1878, at Mohill, and Lord Mountmorres was shot dead on 25 September 1880, near Clonbur, two or three miles from Ashford. Lord Annesley, who had been an MP for Cavan until the 1874 election, wrote Arthur a follow-up to an earlier note. Just in case Arthur hadn't got the message about the threatened murder:

> The information I alluded to, was, that several peers, of whom your lordship was one, were to be shot before Xmas … the name of the late Lord Mountmorres was the first on the list. I therefore thought it well that you should know that such things were being talked of, though I dare say you may already have heard of it.

Unfortunately for Arthur, death threats were really nothing new to him. During the 1872 *Freeman* episode an anonymous writer had dismissed him as 'an orange whelp … as if anybody cared about you or the infernal exhibition', and demanded that he apologise, and contribute to a fund to cover the legal costs of a Galway election candidate, Captain Nolan, who had incurred them losing a case about the Catholic clergy exercising undue influence. Otherwise his life would not be 'worth a month's purchase for we will send you a bullet as well as that scoundrel Keough [*sic*], as we have a person hired to shoot you and him and no mistake'.

The 1880 threat, though, must have felt like a serious one. Six weeks after Arthur received the letter, Captain Boycott and his family finally left. They had to have a military escort out of Lough Mask House, and because no driver could be persuaded to take the reins of the carriage, an army ambulance and driver had to be pressed into service to take them to Claremorris. There they got on a train for Dublin, and put up at the Hammam Hotel for a couple of days before crossing to England. 'He appears very careworn,' reported one newspaper, 'but Mrs Boycott seemed in excellent health and spirits.' She was probably as relieved to have got herself and her husband away from Galway as the tenants were to see them go.

It was obvious by now that life as it had been lived by the landed classes would soon be a thing of the past. Another

Land Act in 1881 sought to rationalise rents and increase assistance for land purchase, and went some way to ameliorating the lives of tenants. Unionist landlords worried about their purses were further unsettled when they saw Home Rule looking more and more likely, and Parnell's influence in restraining violent agitation waning. A Coercion Act was introduced in 1881 and applied with gusto.

In 1882 the new Chief Secretary for Ireland, Frederick Cavendish, was sworn in on 6 May in Dublin. Later that day, as he walked towards the Viceregal Lodge, the Under-Secretary, Thomas Burke, got out of a cab to walk with him. There in the Phoenix Park the two men were stabbed to death by members of a Fenian extremist group, the Invincibles. The murders sent waves of sickened shock through all strata of society, exploded the delicate alliance between Parnell and Gladstone, and pushed out Home Rule by nearly 30 years.

There was nothing straightforward about Arthur's life beyond the brewery, but its plaited strands of marriage, politics, land ownership, philanthropy and the barony represented what he chose to do, and not simply what he had been left to do. He and Olive had no children, and either because or in spite of this, one of Arthur's projects was the rebuilding of the Coombe Lying-in Hospital in the Liberties.

Many couples don't have children, for many reasons, but in Arthur's case this led to speculation that the Ardilauns' was a *mariage blanc*, and that he was not sexually interested in women. That is really neither here nor there. He and Olive enjoyed a long and happy marriage, a relationship of mutual understanding and support, and whether or not this was underpinned by a sexual relationship was their business. He also continued his father's work on the restoration of Archbishop Marsh's Library, beside St Patrick's, and was instrumental in the Dublin Artisans' Dwellings Company, which built affordable housing for the working poor. Even though his personal preferences might have been for shooting parties and titles, he still ploughed his energy, ideas, money and moral support into those parts of Dublin which hungered for them. This, perhaps even more than brewing, was the Guinness family business.

Adelaide and Ned in fancy dress for a ball at St Stephen's Green.

TEN

ENOUGH TO MAKE
US ALL STARE

Arthur's payments for his share of the brewery were due to complete by the middle of 1880. As already seen, the profits were surging. By 1883 they had more than doubled, from £102,000 in 1868 to £230,000. Even this statistic does not quite represent the dramatic growth, as there were five years when profits topped £300,000, with a peak of £399,000 in 1882. Over those 16 years, the brothers between them drew just about half of the brewery's accumulated profits.

Through the years of their joint ownership, they had generally (in 1869 and in 1871–74) drawn similar amounts each year. Some years were anomalous: in 1868, the first year of their joint ownership, Ned drew £2,000 while Arthur drew £42,000. In 1875, Ned drew £3,000, while Arthur drew £105,000, and in the last year of the partnership, 1876, Ned drew £40,000 and Arthur £80,000. These two much larger sums going to Arthur at the end of the partnership knocked the brothers' individual incomes out of balance with one another and brought the totals over the eight years they worked together to £385,000 for Ned, and £530,000 for Arthur. Together these sums amounted to about 60 per cent of the £1.6 million profits over the period, leaving plenty to reinvest in the business.

Year	Sales in Hogsheads	Profit (£)	Drawn by Edward (£)	Drawn by Arthur (£)	Total Drawn (£)
1868	236,000	102,000	2,000	42,000	44,000
1869	266,000	147,000	10,000	10,000	20,000
1870	285,000	151,000	116,000	70,000	186,000
1871	321,000	193,000	67,000	70,000	137,000
1872	365,000	150,000	53,000	58,000	111,000
1873	378,000	134,000	34,000	33,000	67,000
1874	426,000	143,000	60,000	62,000	122,000
1875	489,000	181,000	3,000	105,000	108,000
1876	525,000	302,000	40,000	80,000	120,000
1877	545,000	224,000	66,000	–	66,000
1878	552,000	240,000	27,000	–	27,000
1879	564,000	363,000	30,000	–	30,000
1880	624,000	319,000	159,000	–	154,000
1881	638,000	384,000	326,000	–	326,000
1882	732,000	399,000	440,000	–	440,000
1883	627,000	230,000	35,000	–	35,000
	7,573,000	3,662,000	1,344,000	530,000	1,874,000

It may be blunt to summarise it thus, but it seems that while the partnership survived, Ned both worked harder at the brewery and took less from it. This was the 'anxious work' at which he had not wanted to spend the best years of his life, but he was not a man capable of engaging in any project at half speed. The result was that he worked daily when he was in Dublin, and obtained daily briefings from Purser when he was not, and at the same time he was also constantly turning over ideas as to how to improve and expand.

The approach that Ned had been taught by his father was that even, or perhaps particularly, when profits were increasing, as much money as possible should go back into the business.

The aim was to keep its capital value high and make sure that improvements and expansion plans could be accommodated. And they were: the purchase and development of the land between the old brewery and the river, the construction of the internal railway across both sites, and the acquisition of more storage and modernised machinery were all achieved during the 1870s.

Crucially, this was also a time of investment in the welfare of the brewery workers. For Dubliners, this was the hallmark of the brewery as much as the morning air scented with toasting barley, or the cream and dark amber of the stout itself. A job in the brewery meant security and a decent wage, and brought with it an ever-increasing array of health, social and financial benefits for workers and their families. Ned and Arthur had, during the partnership years, together introduced some early measures, starting with a free dispensary supplying treatment and medicines not just for brewery workers but for their families too. They oversaw the development of a pioneering health and welfare service, with a visiting doctor assisted by a chemist, and a Lady Visitor who made home visits, including to workers' widows (for all the workers were men, until the twentieth century).

Soon a midwife was also recruited to attend to the wives of workers. This recalls the first Olivia Guinness's 21 confinements. Post-partum infection was still common, and though the incidence of maternal mortality was dropping, it was still a danger, and the expertise of a midwife could make all the difference not just at the birth, but afterwards. The comprehensive supports of which the men could and did avail themselves ranged from house-hunting to bridging loans to marriage counselling. From the brewery's point of view, as expressly phrased in the annual medical report of 1884, a happy, healthy worker was a productive worker, less likely to be absent through illness, more likely to live longer and continue to support his family. But the workforce was so large and the benefits so varied that the effects of the Guinness welfare policy seeped out right across the city.

The 1884 report noted that 'our constant efforts to ameliorate the unhealthy environment to your labourers, particularly with regard to their housing, is producing excellent and far-reaching results'. In Dublin matters had not improved much since Annie Lee had been first struck by the desperate poverty she saw, and the Halls' description of the overfilled tenement houses of the Liberties. The Guinnesses' understanding that workers' housing mattered was not unique, but not everyone was in a position to go even some distance to remediate the situation.

The year 1872 saw the construction of Belview Buildings, a workers' housing development close to the brewery, and Ned continued the work alone after Arthur left. In 1882 Rialto Buildings, a similar development further away but still on brewery property, were completed. A couple of years later Lord William Compton called the attention of the Commissioners of the Housing of the Working Classes to these exemplary developments:

> I do not know whether anyone has heard of the buildings which have been put up by Mr Guinness at his brewery in Dublin. To my mind they are the best buildings I have seen.

When the Commissioners visited Ireland, Ned gave evidence, describing the apartments provided by the firm for its workers: one- or two-bedroomed flats with a living room, scullery, water supply and water closet. There were six family cottages too, with three bedrooms apiece. Rents averaged about an eighth of the earnings of the head of family, and the properties were inspected periodically. This kind of arrangement is threaded through with paternalism, that Victorian speciality, but the brewery was reflective, and an internal memo of 1883 acknowledged that the matter of inspections was 'a very delicate and difficult one, and unless great tact and caution is exercised more harm than good may be done'.

As well as housing and health benefits, brewery workers had the advantages of pension provision, sick pay, an allocation of paid holidays and funeral allowances. While the well-being of workers did benefit the brewery, that was not the only motive for the extensive social welfare programme rolled out from the 1870s on, as is borne out by the family history of philanthropy, and by Ned's own philanthropic projects outside the brewery, of which more will be seen in the next chapter.

Ned was not without political ambition. He had withdrawn his candidacy as an MP in 1869, and as the correspondence between Arthur and Isaac Butt in the 1870s records, his standing had been proposed again. His ambition did not extend to making a career as a parliamentarian, but at the end of the nineteenth century it was common for MPs not to be full-time, to be landowners like Arthur or businessmen like Ned, who had a particular cause or interest to promote or defend. While there were naturally those who were dedicating their lives and careers to politics, it was possible to take it on as a part-time job. It could be made to work, from a practical point of view, given that it fitted neatly into the calendar of preoccupations.

There was no autumn session: the House of Commons did not sit between the opening of the grouse season on 12 August and the start of the London season in February. The cachet of being an MP was considerable, as Martelli outlined in 1957:

> an MP's position carried much more consideration than it does today. Membership was confined to a comparatively small social class and the House of Commons was considered the best club in London. To belong to it, like belonging to any exclusive body, put the seal on a man's success in his own sphere, and enhanced his reputation and his influence. He also had the satisfaction of being in the centre of things in London and knowing what went on in the world of politics.

As this language is exclusively male, it is worth mentioning that there was no female MP at Westminster until 1918.

What everyone knew was that, if you had your eye on a title, the surest way to it was by party support, and securing party support meant giving money. A significant party donor whose character was beyond reproach, and whose achievements were such as to be consistent with an honour, could reasonably expect to be given one. So it was not unusual for a man in Ned's position to turn his thoughts to politics. He was independent now, in a way he had never been before. He no longer had to pay any heed to the opinions of his father or his eldest brother.

There seems, despite their fundamental attachment, to have been an undercurrent of tension, or at least competition, between Ned and Arthur, mirroring their wives' relationship. However keen Ned was to help Arthur distance himself from the brewery, the implications cannot have escaped him. Arthur's choice to leave meant that Ned had to stay, and even if Ned's staying had been an active choice, it was one that Arthur rejected. Arthur was the head of the family, the social toast of the town, the guardian of his father's legacy at St Patrick's, the benefactor of the people of Dublin who thought of him every time they crossed the Green. His wife was gifted creatively, an accomplished watercolourist and horticulturalist, an aristocrat by birth, and by marriage richer than any woman in Britain or Ireland except for the queen.

Ned and Adelaide by no means made a poor comparison: they were a similarly rich, gorgeous and capable couple, and with the social golden touch. But Ned was a quieter and more introspective character than his brother, described by his daughter-in-law Gwendolen years later as kind, courteous and modest. 'Despite his abilities and his great riches he was the least conceited of men,' she said.

In 1885 he was appointed the representative of the monarch, as Dublin's High Sheriff. This meant that, when the Prince and Princess of Wales visited Ireland that April, Ned was central to the preparations. It was a sticky enough time for a royal visit, given how turbulent things had been politically in recent years, but Ned was understandably keen for things to go well on his watch. Their visit to Dublin was, he said to the magistrates of Dublin, 'not merely one of Pomp and Pleasure but that their coming is a courageous and sagacious act of Public Service'. The members of Dublin Corporation had little interest in the visit but Ned set up a Citizens' Committee and persuaded Richard Martin, the President of the Chamber of Commerce, to act as chairman, while he himself took the vice-chairmanship.

The royal couple arrived in Ireland, and it rained almost the entire time. The prince was barely able to speak because of a cold. Ten thousand children who had been rounded up to cheer for the royals had to wait outdoors on the cricket ground by the Viceregal Lodge for over an hour, and got drenched. The prince and princess went to the races at Punchestown, Ned and Adelaide's favourite day out, and got lashed on again.

However, a glorious ball cheered everyone up. This was not at the Mansion House, as on previous occasions, but at the Royal Dublin Society in Ballsbridge, where an immense crowd of six or seven thousand guests danced the night away in their best clothes. The prince wore a field-marshal's uniform, and the princess a dress of green velvet over a skirt of pale green satin and silver gauze, fastened with bouquets of shamrock and lilies of the valley. The dancing opened with a royal quadrille: Adelaide danced with the Prince of Wales; Ned danced with Countess Spencer, the wife of the Lord Lieutenant; Richard Martin danced with the Princess of Wales; and Mrs Martin danced with Lord Spencer. It was all marvellous, and nobody had to think about anything unpleasant that had occurred on the tour, like the audible hisses outside Dublin Castle, the angry crowd at the station in Mallow and the combined groaning and hissing in Cork city.

Spencer was relieved that the visit overall had passed off well, and he was particularly happy with the role Ned had played.

A fortnight after the royal couple had left, Gladstone wrote to offer Ned a baronetcy 'in recognition not only of your high position in Ireland but especially of your marked services rendered by you on the important occasion of the visit recently paid to that country by the Prince and Princess of Wales'. The letter waited for Ned at Grosvenor Place for a couple of days, and he apologised for his delay in writing back to the prime minister to gratefully accept the honour.

Poor Ned now had a slight panic about how to proceed – should he thank the queen's private secretary? One of Adelaide's family was Walter Campbell, a ranger at Windsor, and he gave kind and detailed advice:

> I think I would suggest asking the Prince of Wales to express your gratitude to the Queen for the great honour conferred on you – this is the wording ... The Queen ... always likes to be thanked & will think all the more of you for so doing & I fancy the Prince is the one to thank for you, particularly as you got your honour for looking after him. Ask him when you meet him, not any member of his household.

Ned had to be presented to the monarch at the levée, and he asked Annie's brother-in-law David Plunket to be the one to present him. A hasty intervention from Lord Kenmare prevented a faux pas:

> Let me privately tell you that it is usual on such occasions to be presented by the Prime Minister; and that it is likely to be commented on if you depart from that course.

By now it was the morning of the big day, and so Ned wrote immediately to Gladstone's private secretary, Edward Hamilton:

I find I have made a terrible mess about the Levee, not being aware of the etiquette in such matters ... I should have asked the Prime Minister to do me the favour of presenting me.

I beg you to make my apologies to Mr Gladstone for this mistake of mine, which I need not assure you was wholly unintentional, and to ask him to do me the favour of rectifying it by permitting me to have the honour of being presented by him today.

Gladstone was happy to do so, Hamilton replied, and would always remember 'the kind part you played with respect to the matter of private business in which you were connected with him'.

This intriguing little reference was to an episode from two years previously. The board of directors of the Aston Hall Colliery, which included W.H. Gladstone, the prime minister's son, agreed that a loan of £17,000 from Ned, or rather from his business, would be paid back in tonnes of coal. The security was a mortgage on the plant and machinery of the coal mine and associated clay works, at an estimated value of £30,000. When, after two and a half years, £15,000 was still owing on the loan, Ned decided it was time to enforce the break-up sale to recoup his losses.

This matter, like all the brewery affairs, was handled by Ned's trusted solicitor, Fred Sutton. Shortly before the case was due to be heard in the Chancery court Gladstone, via Hamilton, intervened to ask whether Ned would accept some settlement and avoid the break-up sale. The prime minister had either got the wrong end of the stick about some of the facts of the case, or had been misinformed (as he claimed), or was dissembling, but Ned's letters were clear, courteous and firm.

The outcome appears to have been that, before the end of March 1883, Ned did recover £10,000, albeit 'clogged with conditions'. Two-thirds of a bad debt reclaimed was a reasonable outcome for Ned, while for the prime minister and his son it meant avoiding the exposing and embarrassing publicity of a case going ahead. In June 1885 Gladstone remembered that Ned had behaved well, and made a point of acknowledging it.

The royal visit and ensuing baronetcy might have been the height of ambition for some, but not for Ned. He had more to do, and further to go. In 1877, David Plunket had brokered a meeting, the result of which was that Ned was tipped as a potential replacement for the county Dublin MP Colonel Thomas Taylor. It was not until five years later, in October 1882, that Taylor's fellow MP Ian Hamilton wrote to Ned about the possibility of the vacancy 'occurring suddenly', as Taylor was ill: 'You are the friend we have always looked to, as being of all men the one nearly certain to be accepted by the County without opposition.'

Ned replied enthusiastically, although it was 'the most criti-cal moment of the year for my business', and his 'week for buying hops', and so he would not be able to get to Dublin immediately. For all that being an MP could be a part-time job compatible with other interests, there were times when the party's needs had to come first. His competing interests may have told against him. A few months later, in February 1883, Edward King-Harman was the candidate chosen for the upcoming by-election instead of Ned. Lord Crichton referred to King-Harman in a letter to Ned as 'one who will be able to devote more time and attention to his Parliamentary duties than your other avocations would have permitted you to do'.

It seems somewhat rude to have written this in the same letter as a request for £1,000 to pay King-Harman's election expenses, which he could not afford to cover himself. But Ned, even if inwardly he felt disappointed, gamely wrote the cheque and sent it off. A month later a request came for another £500; Ned signed another cheque. Strategising with Plunket, Ned made sure that there was a written record of the party's gratitude, and soon the 1885 general election loomed. Ned wrote a memo outlining the situation of Hamilton, King-Harman and himself all wanting to stand for Dublin County. Ned had never wanted to stand for the City, because it would mean that, when he was at work in St James's Gate, he would have his constituents milling around him. As he observed in March 1884,

> the unpleasantness of it would be very great, for I was always to be found by anyone at St James Gate, not like Arthur who while a member always lived in the country ... if it was put to me in such a way by the leaders of the party I would feel bound to consider it, but if it was only a question of sitting for the City or of never going into the House of Commons at all I would unhesitatingly choose the latter ... I had no wish unduly to press my claims, but that I was placed in a very unpleasant position having lost the thing I had so much looked forward to.

It does seem unfair that, in the party's interest, Ned had stood aside – voluntarily or upon request – for King-Harman, had paid for King-Harman's campaign and still wasn't getting a swing at the ball himself. But if the party did persuade him to stand for the City, their indebtedness would only increase. What exactly that indebtedness warranted as payback remained to be seen. Sir Stafford Northcote wrote and put the request to him. 'I know it is asking a great deal from you; but I trust you may be willing to make the sacrifice.' Ned replied that he could not refuse.

Before matters went any further, Plunket wanted some kind of guarantee for Ned that the prize was in the offing. He wrote to the Conservative leader Lord Salisbury outlining what Ned was prepared to do for the party, including standing for election in a constituency which in no way suited him, and donating more money to party funds. While Plunket did not go into the figures, Ned in fact committed to a £5,000 donation and a follow-up to the same tune, bringing his total contributions up to £11,500. To approximate what that represented, when Salisbury's former Under-Secretary for Foreign Affairs, Bourke, went to Madras as Lieutenant Governor in 1886, it was on an annual salary of £12,000.

Salisbury wrote back in plain enough terms, putting into words what no one else had to date. He marked his letter to Plunket of 16 August 1885 'Very Confidential': 'I should say to you that I am not in a condition to promise that "gratitude" means a Peerage – at all events as yet.' Plunket pressed the point now that the word had entered the conversation: 'Guinness does certainly look forward to a Peerage as a natural object of his ambition.'

Salisbury, who was now travelling, had left Plunket's address behind, but asked for a message to be passed to him that 'his letter was quite satisfactory to me', and there the matter had to be shelved for the moment. Ned was appreciative of and moved by Plunket's deft handling of the situation, writing affectionately from Farmleigh that he was 'certainly the best of friends'. A less capable person might have flinched from addressing the man who was about to become prime minister with such directness on a delicate matter.

Ned now had to run the gauntlet of the election campaign. His main opponent was the nationalist Irish Parliamentary Party candidate Edmund Dwyer Gray, a staunch Parnellite and the son of Arthur's old jousting partner, Sir John Gray of the *Freeman's Journal*. The *Freeman* had a field day reporting in the most vivid colour on Gray's rallies and the verbal slingshots fired at Ned. The passionate Home Ruler Tim Healy shot off every barb he could. He praised Gray for being 'a large employer', but when told that Ned was one too, he brushed that off by asking 'do the Guinnesses pay their labourers for doing nothing?' He criticised him for having sold off the Winter Palace, to be taken apart and reconstructed in Battersea Park, and characterised this as evidence that Ned thought of the Irish as 'the brutal Irish, the drunken Irish – drunken on my own stout – ... the savage Irish'.

Ned had sold the government the main exhibition building for use by the Royal University of Ireland (later the National University of Ireland), and the 1882 Exhibition of Irish Manufactures had been held in a purpose-built centre in Rutland Square. This, Healy sneered, was because 'the idea of anything Irish except porter flourishing in this country was too much for him'. Ned was said to be a friend of the working man, but Healy noticed 'about election times a sporadic rash breaking out like pimples all over the face of Ireland, the shape of friends of the working man'. And Ned was tainted by Arthur's shambolic election experience in 1869, as the *Freeman's Journal* was only too keen to point out:

> The Guinnesses were represented as being the family who made a present to the city of the park in Stephen's-green. Well, all the odour of the flowers and all the smell of the trees in that park would not be sufficient to perfume and to purify the memory of the corruption with which the Guinnesses deluged the city fifteen years ago.

Ned was not constitutionally suited to public mud-slinging, and did not respond with similar public speeches to huge crowds, though he did make one at the Antient Concert Rooms on Great Brunswick Street (now Pearse Street) shortly before the vote took place. He was mild and modest in his approach, and did not prolong the engagement by dealing with every criticism which had been levelled at him. He did firmly rebuff one accusation, which was that he was an Orangeman, stemming from the fact that he and Arthur had both contributed to the building of an Orange hall in Rutland Square.

> I am not and never have been an Orangeman. I have subscribed to an Orange hall, and I am not ashamed of having done so. [*Cheers.*] Though I am not a Catholic –

> [*cheers*] – it is equally true that I have subscribed to many
> Catholic institutions – [*great cheering*] – and I am proud
> of having done so. [*Renewed cheering.*]

The *Freeman* continued to refer to him as an Orange candidate, and as one doing battle 'for the Ascendancy'. Given his
fundamental reluctance, Ned probably experienced some sense
of relief when in the heel of the hunt he lost the election to
Gray. He had done what the party had asked of him, including
showing he was prepared to serve it as a candidate, and ponying
up significant amounts of money, but did not actually have to
embark on the awkwardness of life of an MP. As it happened,
the seat was vacated in 1888 when Gray died unexpectedly,
aged only 43, but despite some noises being made by the Lord
Lieutenant, Lord Londonderry, about Ned returning to the fray,
Plunket, ever Ned's most judicious advisor in these matters,
counselled caution.

> I should be very careful ... not to take any other tone
> except that nothing but the strongest pressure from the
> Government would induce you in the present circum-
> stances to stand.

He did not stand, but he kept his cheques coming, bringing his total
contributions over the ten years from 1880 to at least £30,000.

Brewery matters were still calling, and the time had now
come for Ned to put into operation the intention which he had
been developing privately for some time. This was his plan to sell
the brewery. Ned had confided in Plunket, but played his cards
otherwise close to his chest, though he had spoken to Nathaniel
Rothschild about it as far back as 1879. One of the arguments
Ned marshalled in favour of selling was that he found the work
and responsibility just too taxing. He had often previously
referred to business worries taxing his health, and no one could

argue with his wanting to prioritise it, nor doubt that being in sole charge of an organisation of the brewery's size generated a huge amount of stress.

In 1885 Ned opened discussion with Edward Baring of the London banking house Baring Brothers. Baring had been raised to the peerage with a barony that year, and was now Lord Revelstoke. He advised against an outright sale and recommended flotation on the Stock Exchange, a process which Barings would manage. Ned wanted to stay involved with the brewery, and explained as much to the heads of department at St James's Gate, whose staff were naturally uncertain not just about whether their jobs and the way they went about them were likely to change, but also about whether in a new régime the famously generous and reliable employee welfare system would survive. He first explained his concerns for his health, and went on to describe his intention to retain a majority holding in the new company, and to return as chairman of the board even after his obligatory three-year term was long over.

> I have felt extremely reluctant to sever my connection with the brewery and to surrender my interest in the welfare of those with whom I have been so long associated. I have accordingly arranged that I shall be chairman of the company, retaining a substantial interest in the undertaking.

This language suggests that Ned knew he would find it hard to live without the brewery which had formed the background to his thoughts for so long. To look at it from a slightly different angle, he got something from the brewery that he didn't get from being involved in any other project. There were many ways in which he might have addressed the strain placed on his health by his running the brewery single-handedly, but Ned was now answerable only to himself, and of course to Adelaide, who must have been happy to think that her husband could reduce the wear and tear on himself while sacrificing none of his income. On the contrary, he would increase it.

The brewery had been in private, family ownership now for 130 years, and was, as one newspaper put it, 'in the full tide of its enormous development'. It was the largest brewery in the world and had showed an average annual profit of almost £500,000 over the previous five years. Astonishingly for an organisation operating in the credit economy of the late nineteenth century, almost all sales, except those to the oldest and most trusted customers, were for cash, meaning that the usual array of bad debts was simply not a factor. In 1885, with sales of well over £2 million, bad debts ran at under £3,000. Property was almost all held freehold, and there were no mortgages.

The valuation of the company was initially estimated at £5 million, increased at Ned's insistence to £6 million. But even that valuation proved to be low, for Ned did not foresee the ravenous appetite the public would show when faced with the prospect of getting their hands on Guinness shares. When the prospectus was published in October 1886 it was the first glimpse anyone outside the brewery had had of just how good the figures were. No one had realised just how beautifully and profitably the place was run. In London the *Globe* newspaper expressed real surprise that

> a brewery which turns out nothing but brown beer is doing a far larger business than the great Burton firms. Here, in London, the popular taste has undergone a great change in this particular, brown beer having been largely replaced by ale, while it was believed that Bass and Allsopp had effected the same revolution abroad. This is clearly not the case, or the demand for Guinness's famous stout would have diminished, instead of increasing by leaps and bounds up to the present date.

The subscription lists officially opened on Monday 25 October 1886 and were due to remain open until the deadline of 4 pm the next day, but the surge of applications was so overwhelming that the lists had to be closed after an hour. In fact, names had been added to the lists ever since the prospectus had been published on the Saturday. Even those lucky enough to get their names in were not able to get all the shares they wanted. The physical pressure of the dense crowd of would-be applicants at the Barings office in Bishopsgate Street in the City of London was such that one of the outer doors was broken, and this despite the police guard.

No one in the City was talking of anything else. The *Evening Standard* was open-mouthed:

> The fact that the applications for the Shares of Messrs. Guinness and Co. reached the nominal total of about a hundred millions is enough to make us all stare ... The subscription list was not advertised to open before yesterday [Monday] morning but by noon on Saturday it was computed that the whole of the five million two hundred thousand pounds demanded had been applied for twenty times over. Still the tide flowed on, and yesterday morning – when the list was opened for a moment *pro forma* – there must have been enough money offered to buy the businesses of thirty Guinness's Breweries.

In fact very few of the public were able to get the shares they wanted. The possibilities for public involvement were always likely to be limited, given that a couple of million pounds' worth of shares were sewn up for individuals in the golden circle of Barings and certain other banks. Even Ned's own circle didn't benefit to the same tune as the bankers: Arthur's allocation was only £15,000. There was talk of sharp practice. *Money* magazine analysed the allocations and determined that more than 50 per cent of the shares had gone to those involved in the flotation, creating a profit of over £1.5 million for the golden circle, or 'inner ring', as once the markets opened, the preference shares shot up by 25 per cent and the ordinary shares by 75 per cent.

Ned himself could have made even more than the immense amount of money he did make. This still totted up to well over £4 million even after he had taken care of substantial gifts to his brother Lee (£150,000), his sister Annie (£52,000) and David Plunket (£10,000), and had looked after the brewery workers. He gave the brewers ordinary shares to the value of three months' salary 'as a slight mark of my sense of the valuable services which you have so kindly rendered to me in the past', sent cheques to the clerks, and arranged for the tradesmen and labourers to receive a bonus of four weeks' pay.

Barings had recommended that Ned fill the new board with as many Guinnesses as possible: 'The more Guinnesses the better; all Guinnesses if you can manage it'. But other than Ned in the chair, there were only two, neither of whom was Arthur. Claude Guinness was now *in situ* as managing director, and would stay on in that role. He was Adelaide's brother, and thus a direct descendant of the first Arthur's brother Samuel. Another brother of theirs, Reginald Guinness, was also on the board, along with Ned's friend Viscount Castlerosse, two bankers, Henry Glyn and Herman Hoskier, and Dublin solicitor James Stewart.

These new arrangements were not to Mr Purser's taste. He had been working at St James's Gate now for over 60 years, perfecting the product and managing brewery affairs. He knew it inside out. He had never worked by answering to a board of bankers, and he had no wish to start doing so now. Ned wrote to him at the end of November 1886 to offer him a parting present of 500 shares, half preference and half ordinary, 'which I beg of you to receive not for its intrinsic value, but as a memento of your long connection with the business'.

Mr Purser declined. He had his years of 'centage', which was an agreed percentage on each barrel of beer brewed, on deposit with the brewery and would take that with the interest it had accrued, as he was entitled to do. Ned wrote back enclosing it, in the form of 'a cheque for £217,196, which discharges my obligation to you under the heads of Deposit and working Blotter accounts and three months' interest less income tax'. The letter was pure business, and was a rather cool and formal conclusion to an extraordinarily long and beneficial relationship.

Other members of the Purser family did get involved: William Purser Geoghegan, head brewer, got £5,000 of shares, and his brother Samuel, head engineer, got £2,000. John Tertius Purser lived for seven years after his retirement from the brewery. He died at home in Rathfarnham Castle in April 1893, and was buried in the Moravian Cemetery there. His assets when he died amounted to £211,000, nearly all of the money he had been paid from his brewery deposits.

The old guard had almost all gone, and the brewery had made the transition to the new era. It was time for Ned, too, to find his feet in a new world of his own.

A shooting party at Elveden in January 1901. Ned stands third from left, beyond the steering wheel; Walter and Ernest lean on the front tyres; Adelaide sits in the top row, in profile. Bottom centre is Prince Victor Duleep Singh, son of Elveden's previous owner.

ELEVEN

THE EDWARDIAN AGE

Ned was about to turn 40, and had already achieved a huge amount since his father's death. In his commercial life, he had steered the brewery through partnership, into a period of sole ownership, and through its flotation on the Stock Exchange. In his family life, he had married a woman he loved and who loved him, and their marriage had given them three children, because as well as my great-grandfather Rupert, Ned and Adelaide had had two more sons, Ernest and Walter.

At the time of the flotation, the boys were aged ten, eight and six. Ned had a good relationship with his sister Annie and her family, and while there could be intermittent spikiness between himself and Arthur, as had been evident since the early 1870s, their relationship had survived a number of challenges. Life was good and looked likely to continue so. The pressure of work was dramatically reduced, home life was happy and there was plenty of money, as well as more time and energy, for the personal and philanthropic projects he was constantly bringing to fruition.

In the wake of the success of the housing schemes which Ned had instigated for the workers at St James's Gate, he began thinking about the creation of sorely needed housing schemes for people beyond the brewery circle. He planned to build blocks of flats in the areas of London and Dublin where the least privileged lived. The rental income from these flats would be worked back into the scheme so that more could be built. It was a similar model of self-perpetuation to that which he had used in the brewery, reinvesting profits for the benefit of the business itself. With this in mind, he founded the Guinness Trust, and appointed three trustees, who were David Plunket; Scottish businessman and MP Charles Ritchie; and Lord Rowton.

Rowton, a nephew of the great factory reformer Lord Shaftesbury, was chairman. Like Ned, he thoroughly enjoyed the life of a rich man, while carrying with him always the belief that the natural order of things made it incumbent on him to help as much as possible those who had less than they needed, or were otherwise suffering. As well as the Guinness Trust housing, the Rowton Houses in London provided a kind of hostel accommodation for men, intended to be a step up from lodging houses. This was replicated in Dublin with the Iveagh House Hostel. This still operates today (now known simply as the Iveagh Hostel), offering secure accommodation to men experiencing homelessness, and is run by the Iveagh Trust, a separate body established to take over the Guinness Trust's work in Dublin.

The trust Ned set up on 2 April 1890 was to the value of £250,000, of which £200,000 was for a London Fund and the rest for a Dublin Fund. As the secretary to the trust, Lees Knowles MP, put it in a letter to the Lord Mayor of Dublin in January 1890,

> the Guinness Trustees have had placed at their disposal a sum of £50,000, to be expended by them in building dwellings for the poorer section of the working classes of Dublin, whose wants have not been met by existing agencies.

In accordance with the family's generally non-sectarian spirit, Ned made it explicit that religious division would have no place in the work of the trust, and that religion would play no part in determining who might benefit from it. The trust acquired sites at Thomas Court behind James's Street, where it built Thomas Court Buildings; to the south of St Patrick's Cathedral on Kevin Street, which linked St Stephen's Green with Patrick Street; and to the north of the cathedral an adjoining site which was to be cleared and laid out as a public park. Families whose homes were demolished to make way for St Patrick's Park were rehomed in three of the 14 new Kevin Street blocks, completed by 1901.

In the interim, the New Year's Honours list of 1891 created Ned a baron. This was now clearly warranted, regardless of his party donations and readiness to put aside his own preferences and stand for election, by his achievements in business and his wholehearted approach to philanthropy. Ned was thrilled, and deeply honoured. The press found it very easy to produce colourful copy in reporting the news of the 'porter peer', as always unable to resist the combination of beer, riches and a glamorous life. As the *Truth* put it:

> The new Lord is principally celebrated for the excellence of his stout, for the munificent gifts of a quarter of a million of money towards the better housing of the poor of London and Dublin, and for possessing a three thousand guinea sofa.

Others couldn't resist punning, with plenty of regional papers recycling the remark that Ned, 'known in the "beerage" as Guinness, will sink all memories of stout in the peerage under the title of Lord Farmleigh'.

In fact Farmleigh was not the title Ned chose, nor was another early runner, St Patrick's. In the end he plumped for Iveagh, the territory of the Magennis family in Down, based on a family belief that the Guinnesses were descended from Magennis. The Magennises were Catholics who raised two regiments for the Jacobites at the Battle of the Boyne. When King James was defeated, they went into exile, first in Austria, later France and then Spain, and King William stripped them of the title of viscounts of Iveagh, which they had held for nearly a hundred years.

Sir Bernard Burke, Ulster King of Arms and Keeper of the State Papers, wrote to Ned that even were anyone still to lay claim to the existing Iveagh title, it would make no odds: 'There would simply be a VISCOUNT MAGENNIS and a BARON IVEAGH, the former a Viscounty of Ireland – the latter, a Barony of the United Kingdom.' So reassured and guided, Ned became Baron Iveagh of Iveagh. His choice was to identify himself and his family with Ireland, and with this old Irish association, rather than with something more modern of his own creation, like Farmleigh or Elveden.

With the brewery sold, and a peerage attained, the third big change for Ned and Adelaide was finding and buying Elveden, an estate on the border between Suffolk and Norfolk. Ned had in 1888 first opened purchase negotiations with Prince Duleep Singh, formerly Maharaja of the Punjab and, incidentally, the former owner of the Koh-i-Noor diamond. He had ended up in exile in Britain as a young man after his kingdom was annexed by the East India Company.

The property ownership was mired in political difficulties revolving around the India Office's purchase of it as a residence for Duleep Singh, Singh's move to Paris and subsequent attempt to relinquish it, and the eventual formation of a trust. After six years of dreadful heel-dragging and flip-flopping on the vendor's side, Ned all but completed the purchase instead of a different estate, Savernake, from the Marquess of Ailesbury. This transaction became mired too, in two years of correspondence and a court case. But all of a sudden Duleep Singh died. The trustees contacted Ned immediately. The sale was on, and he bought it in April 1894 for £160,000.

Elveden estate had fallen into considerable neglect during Duleep Singh's years of absence, but the heath and woods of which it was largely made up were perfect for shooting, which Ned loved, and around which so much of the country hospitality of his circle revolved. The estate covered about 17,000 acres, soon increased to 23,000. Of this, 7,000 were allocated as farmland, although it was not particularly fertile or profitable land; 2,400 acres were woods and plantations; and the rest was warren and heath. The better fields were given over to barley, which would have satisfied the first Arthur Guinness, others to a corn–roots–corn–clover rotation, and Suffolk sheep munched their way around the rest.

The house had started as a fairly straightforward Georgian manor, with an appealing-sounding skylit library, but Duleep Singh had rebuilt it into a luxurious mansion, with Italianate exteriors and exquisite marble interiors modelled on a Mughal palace. The Iveaghs greatly expanded Elveden Hall, with architectural plans drawn up by William and Clyde Young, who had designed significant government buildings in Whitehall, and the neighbouring estate, Culford Hall, for the Earls Cadogan.

They added a symmetrical extra wing and a magnificent connecting central hall of white Carrera marble, rising through four storeys to the roof and a copper-covered dome, which echoed the Mughal arches and columns of Duleep Singh's house. Ned and Adelaide had never visited India, but they employed as their designer Sir Caspar Purdon Clarke. Born in Dublin, he had not only visited India, but was Director of the South Kensington Museum in London (later renamed the Victoria and Albert Museum), and an interiors specialist. He was overseer of the India Museum collection, which had started on the premises of the East India Company in Leadenhall Street in 1798, and whose 20,000 artefacts had been amalgamated into the South Kensington Museum collections.

Sir Caspar created one of the most extraordinary rooms in England, incorporating decorative elements which drew on the British Museum's collection of plaster casts. Adding to the splendid drama of the whole were two giant marble fireplaces, beaten copper doors and galleries around three sides of the central hall. The fireplaces were for effect only, as the real heat came from a modern central heating system. The echo of the marble was softened with Adelaide's favourite decoration, flowers, and gorgeous fabrics, making the hall a favourite room for all kinds of entertainment from tea parties to card games to concerts. In a modern echo, it has recently been used for summer opera.

It took a considerable staff to keep the place and its occupants clean, warm, dressed and fed. Some, including a talented pastry chef, a Frenchman, travelled with the family as they moved between homes. At Elveden the staff were accommodated in a separate new wing of two storeys. Here there were bedrooms allocated to the butler, footman-in-waiting, groom of the chambers, under-butler, housekeeper, cook, lady's maids and valet, as well as 30 bedrooms for other staff.

The wing included a kitchen, a scullery, the cook's store, four larders, a serving room, the kitchen maids' room, a plate room, two pantries, two brushing rooms, a flower room, a linen room, a still room, a china closet, a knife room, a boot room, the servants' hall and a dispensary. These were the house staff, but of course there were all the outdoor workers too, and this did not just mean grooms and gardeners. It meant 76 staff in the game department alone, including gamekeepers, under keepers and warreners. As head keeper Ned and Adelaide made sure to retain Tom Turner, who had been employed at Elveden by Duleep Singh, and knew the estate so well.

Ned's shooting parties were characterised not only by the sport itself but by the warmth and ease of the couple's hospitality in and out of the house. Rather like those beautifully catered lunches at Punchestown, hot food was served at properly laid tables standing on floorboards, and protected from the elements by marquees. In another example of using indoor comforts outdoors, the group photographs which were often taken and kept in the shooting records were posed on huge carpets flung across the grass. Even dinner could be served outdoors, the night illuminated by special electric lamps, with umbrellas at the ready, although the ladies' hats were broad enough to serve anyway.

The Prince of Wales (the future Edward VII), whom Ned and Adelaide had entertained in the Dublin rain in 1885, became a frequent guest, and is pictured in the family photograph albums. So too his son, the future George V, when he was Prince of Wales, would often go to stay. Duleep Singh's sons, Prince Victor and Prince Frederick Duleep Singh, were also invited. Rupert was already 20 when his parents bought Elveden, his brothers 18 and 16, and all three of them shot alongside Victor. Not everyone who was included in the parties did shoot, and guns were usually limited to about eight, or six if the Prince of Wales were in the group.

In October 1896, for example, Ned and Adelaide invited about 20 people. The photograph shows a varied group, including the hotelier and philanthropist William Waldorf Astor, as yet neither a British subject nor a peer; Lord Rowton, already at work on the Guinness Trust with Ned; Lionel and Victoria Sackville-West, whose daughter Vita, then four and a half, would grow up to become the famous writer and gardener; Lord and Lady Granby, he in vivid plaid with what look like hare skins thrown around his shoulders; Ireland's Lord Chief Justice, Lord Morris, and Lady Morris; Derek Keppel, equerry to the Duke of York; Norfolk neighbour and Liberal politician Lord Suffield, and his daughter Judith Harbord; and Lord Rathmore, as David Plunket had become.

Of these, Granby, Rathmore, Keppel, Sackville-West and Ned were the only guns. The photograph demonstrates the range of Ned and Adelaide's circle, encompassing Ireland and England, business and philanthropy, law and politics, new neighbours and old friends. When considered with other photographs in the albums, this one gives insights into the characters of both Ned and Adelaide. When he appears in photographs, which is not all the time, Ned remains somewhat in the background, never placing himself centrally or to the fore. Adelaide's preference was to be photographed, as she appears here, in profile, and photographs of her in any other pose are rare.

The whole thing was so well-run that on one occasion in 1904 when Lord Savile was asked down, he wrote to Ned with a special request:

May I bring a keeper with me to show him how things
ought to be done? If you would rather I didn't please say
so frankly and also whether I shall bring a dog. So looking
forward to my visit.

Ned didn't have to think twice: 'Of course we can put him up.'
The views of the keeper are not recorded.

The albums create an extraordinarily vivid statistical,
visual and personal record of those three-day parties: tiring days
outdoors, a reviving drink by the fire, then chatty dinners from
which guests slipped away one by one to sleep soundly on starched
sheets. Meanwhile in the servants' wing someone brushed down
their clothes and got the mud out of their boots. The bags were
counted and recorded. The next day, another couple of hundred
partridge, another couple of thousand pheasant, more chat, more
ideas, another project taking shape.

Ned and Adelaide did not live at Elveden full-time. They
moved between Farmleigh, St Stephen's Green and Grosvenor
Place too, fortunate to have so many comfortable homes, all
of which were places where their friends and family gathered.
They were lucky, too, that home life, whichever home they
found themselves in, had always been happy. Before the century
turned, they had had the satisfaction of watching three boys
reach adulthood. They were sent to Eton, like their uncles, and
though their childhoods were traditional, they did not map the
pattern of their father's.

While at 15 Ned had been walking to work at St James's
Gate with Benjamin Lee, the letters home from Rupert show
that even at 18 he was still free to concentrate on school. His
particular interest was rowing, in which Eton took huge pride,
and in which he would continue to excel after leaving school. In
one letter to his father, written in May 1892, of the eight short
paragraphs, seven were devoted to rowing and cricket, and the
remaining one was a banal comment on the weather. But all the

boys knew Ireland as well as they knew England, and their many Guinness relations too.

Their uncle Arthur didn't feature much, if at all, in the shooting parties, but then he was still hosting his own at Ashford. Indeed, he hosted the Prince of Wales at a shoot in February 1905, taking him to Ballykine Wood, where the best and most numerous woodcock were, and then to the islands in Lough Mask for snipe and duck. A full technical report, with every movement of the beaters and the birds, was published in the *Irish Field*, along with photographs. The Irish visit was as usual a busy one, and in Dublin the Prince of Wales attended the first levée of the season, at which Ned and Arthur were also present, as were the three young Guinness brothers.

Before leaving the capital the prince visited the new Exhibition of Modern Art Pictures at the Dublin Museum. It was the precursor to the city's modern art gallery, still a few years off. This was the special project of Sir Hugh Lane, who intended to give his personal collection, including works by Corot, Ingres, Monet, Degas, Courbet, Renoir and Pissarro, to the city. Lane identified a site in St Stephen's Green on which he could build the gallery a permanent home. It was behind the statue of Arthur which had been erected in 1891, and when the Board of Works put the proposal to Arthur he flatly vetoed the plan. Olive Ardilaun did donate two pictures to Lane's project, and Ned donated three: *Lilacs*, by Millais; *Pretty Lucy Bond* by G.F. Watts; and *Venetian Scene* by James Holland.

A row about the building of the gallery went on for some years, with opponents arguing that public money would be better spent on sorting out the continuing housing crisis, and proponents saying that the gallery would be a boon to the poor given that there was little opportunity to see these kinds of paintings other than in the houses of the rich. Lane died on the *Lusitania* in 1915, and an unwitnessed codicil to his will left his collection to Dublin to form the core of a collection to be held by the

Municipal Gallery of Modern Art. But the original will had left them to the National Gallery in London and by the 1950s the paintings were still there. Bryan Guinness, Ned's grandson, urged the British government in 1953 to return the collection to Dublin, and from 1959 an agreement was brokered to share and rotate the paintings between London and Dublin.

There were still projects like this modern art gallery for Arthur and Ned to discuss, still some shared property interests, and still some shared passions like shooting, but by now the brothers had a manageable rather than a close relationship. When Ned was made a Knight of St Patrick in 1895, Arthur's feathers were definitely ruffled. The honour came from Lord Salisbury, prime minister once again, who must have remembered Ned's hefty contributions to the party some years before. Arthur considered Salisbury to have betrayed the cause of the Conservative party.

By now the Iveaghs and the Salisburys had become friends, and Rupert had a particular friendship with Salisbury's private secretary Schomberg McDonnell, a son of the tenth Earl of Antrim and a fellow Old Etonian, known to his schoolfriends as 'Pom', and described by the *Sketch* as the most ideal right-hand man a prime minister ever had. In time he would act as best man at Rupert's wedding. Letters flew between the Iveaghs and the Salisburys with the informal ease of people who saw each other often: 'If it is the same to you we will bring our maid down with us'; 'we both look back with the greatest pleasure on our yachting trip'; 'if you have done all your shooting & have nothing better to do on the 28th inst will you & Ld. Iveagh come here for a day or two? We shall be very glad to see you!'; 'the photographs are charming and shall go into my book at once!'; 'many thanks for a fine haunch of venison which has just arrived here!'; 'thank you for having taken the trouble to enquire and let us know about the villas to let near Turbie-sur-mer'.

The four were in each other's company so often, and communication between them was so easy, that an understanding about whether or not Ned was interested in becoming a Knight of St Patrick might easily have arisen. The situation was completely unlike the one only four years previously in which David Plunket had with such delicate force raised with Salisbury the topic of Ned's possible peerage.

Correspondence between Ned's private secretary and Schomberg McDonnell make it clear that the suggestion that Ned be made a Knight of St Patrick originated with the prime minister, and that Ned looked on the honour as 'the very highest any Irishman can aspire to'. As a vacancy had to arise in the order – that is, someone had to die – before a new knight could be invested, there was only room for one, and Ned was chosen, not Arthur.

Lord Rathmore, who knew both brothers so well, predicted in November 1895 the effect of the announcement on Arthur. He wrote to Ned that the more he thought about it, the less he liked the idea of Arthur getting the news of the 'ribband' without an accompanying explanation. He would write to Arthur himself, hoping to 'prevent him assigning to us any deliberate plan upon the subject'. He did this, attempting to soften the blow for Arthur, and while he did so more to protect both himself and Ned from an accusatory response than from simple consideration for Arthur's feelings, it was a typically kind and tactful letter. He opened by saying that Ned had told him the news, and that it had been practically impossible for Ned to refuse, with acceptance required more or less on the spot.

> I knew nothing about it, in fact I had forgotten that Lord Waterford was a KP. But remembering, as I now do, a conversation I once had with you on the subject of such an honour it was <u>most stupid</u> of me not to have thought of it when Waterford died, and asked you whether you would like to take any steps towards putting your claims forward on that occasion!

Ned himself wrote to Arthur a few days later to break the news, suggesting that Arthur would be as surprised as Ned had himself been. Arthur's reply struck a sequence of notes between wounded, petulant and sulky:

> I am not at all 'surprised' to hear of your obtaining the St Patrick's ribbon for David Plunket told me more than a year since that owing to your liberal expenditure for party purposes you had the first claim for one and I think he added for something greater … I have never directly or indirectly asked for it or done anything about it.

He mentioned some ways in which he had not done anything about it: four or five years earlier David Plunket had raised the matter with Lord Limerick, who had swept in and taken the vacancy himself; he had never sought an explanation as to why his contributions to party funds had been suppressed for years in the party list; two years ago he had had another conversation with David Plunket about who might be in the running. The whole thing had scarcely crossed his mind, and this would show Ned 'how little I have thought of such things'. Arthur was in bristling form, saying that, even if he had wanted to, his 'miserable health' prevented him from advertising himself. His party contributions were 'spent in Ireland and on more or less secret undertakings and therefore far from paying (in an honour sense) or flashy […] I could not bring myself to do what some men have done to obtain this honour.'

This letter casts Arthur in a most unattractive light. Life had unquestionably treated him well, and he had worked with his privilege and his many gifts, but he was not at a point of seeing things in the round. One newspaper article, reproduced in several regional papers that November, compared the two brothers, something which in itself probably exasperated Arthur. They had both derived their immense fortunes from the great Guinness Brewery ... They are both philanthropists on a millionaire scale, but whereas Lord Ardilaun seldom, if ever, speaks of his connection with the great mercantile house, Lord Iveagh rather glories in it, and sometimes says when giving away hundreds of thousands that the credit is due not to him, but to the merits of Guinness stout.

As boys they had had the same start; as young married men Arthur had seemed to be edging ahead in the game of life. But Arthur's younger, quieter brother had by now outstripped him in so many of the things they both cared about. Social position, material wealth, business success: Ned had done better at everything. He was popular and sociable, holding on to longstanding friends and now counting the prime minister and the Prince of Wales in his circle, and David Plunket, who had been best man at Arthur's wedding, as his best friend. Ashford had always been enviable, described 16 years earlier as having the best sport in the country, but Ned had Elveden now. It seemed that Ned's life continued to open and blossom, while Arthur grew increasingly entrenched and suspicious.

There would be further differences to come, wedging open the gap between the brothers. In 1897 the *Freeman's Journal* reported on 'a somewhat acrimonious discussion between the brothers of the house of Guinness' when Arthur refused an appeal for a donation for new bells for St Patrick's. His argument, which was not without merit, was that his father, 'when he restored the Cathedral at immense cost, took special pride and pleasure in the restoration of the old bells to which he had listened as a child'.

There is something lovely about this echo across time of the first Arthur's era, when Benjamin Lee first became aware of the old cathedral's presence in Dublin. Ned, on the other hand, was happy to donate. 'Lord Ardilaun's younger and richer brother, Lord Iveagh, took a totally different view, and when appealed

to promptly sent a cheque not for a subscription only, but for
the entire cost,' the newspaper explained. At the service of dedication of the new bells, 'Lord Iveagh was present, and Lord
Ardilaun was not'.

A couple of years later Ned donated to the election campaign
costs of Horace Plunkett, a moderate Unionist with a special
interest in technological and other developments in farming,
and a leader of the co-operative movement. Arthur, for whom
moderation in Unionism was no longer acceptable, and who
was president of the Royal Dublin Society, which Plunkett had
criticised for its lack of progress in Irish farming methods, was
having none of it. Nor did he approve of Plunkett's support for
a Catholic University. He and Trinity lecturer Edward Dowden
promptly arranged for another Unionist candidate to stand. The
Unionist vote was split, and neither man was elected.

When the Anglo-Boer War broke out in South Africa in the
autumn of 1899, pro-Boer feeling surged through the city and
spilled into demonstrations and riots, with the Transvaal flag, the
vierkleur, in evidence. But an Irish brigade was raised to fight on
the British side: '[t]hey are all fine, strapping fellows and typical
Celts', an approving report of new recruits said. Ned decided to
put his support into medical aid, and to that end offered to pay
for staffing and equipping a mobile hospital. This civilian operation consisted of 15 wagons, two water carts, two forage carts,
ten marquees to serve as wards, 20 square bell tents to be staff
quarters, plenty of medicines, champagne and brandy for the sick
and wounded, along with supplies of basics like pyjamas, socks,
handkerchiefs and slippers. The hospital was overseen by Sir
William Thomson, a distinguished Belfast surgeon, who had just
completed a term as president of the Royal College of Surgeons
in Ireland, and Rupert was to serve as his assistant.

As well as a medical staff, there was a large ancillary staff,
many of whom came from the brewery to work at compound-
ing prescriptions, doing laundry, cooking and administrative

work, and 15 orderlies who were seconded from the Royal Irish Constabulary. A member of the Dublin Metropolitan Police went along as a farrier, and there were others in the transport division doing everything from driving to harness-making. Annie Maud McDonnell from the Richmond Hospital went as matron, assisted by Miss Walker, both of whom Sir William later singled out for their 'brilliant service and pluck', particularly impressed by the time they travelled from Kroonstad to Pretoria, about 140 miles, 'in an open bogie truck, exposed to bitter weather and the possible attacks of the enemy', rather than waiting for 'the luxury of a passenger train'.

The first personnel and equipment sailed to Cape Town in February 1900. Ned had provided khaki staff uniforms, and the staff were to get free rations as well as their pay. Before they set off from the docks in London, there was an enormous breakfast for the staff, and each was presented with a silver-mounted pipe, inscribed 'Irish Hospital'. Ned, with his usual attention to detail, also made sure that everyone got a pouch of tobacco. By March they reached Naauwport, and by June Pretoria. At first they used their marquees and bell tents, but with 65 of their patients suffering from enteric fever and the weather horribly cold and wet, Sir William got permission from the military governor to use the Palace of Justice as a hospital. They were able to accommodate 500 patients there, and Dr George Stoker carried on at Bloemfontain with six tentfuls of patients from both sides of the conflict. The hospital unit stayed in South Africa until the middle of October, when their remaining patients were put into the care of the Medical Corps.

In his last despatch from South Africa, Field Marshal Lord Roberts, a fellow Knight of St Patrick, mentioned the Irish Hospital and those who raised, equipped and maintained them. In a story which has featured so many men it is interesting that in this military acknowledgement women outnumber men. He named: 'Lord Iveagh, the Honourable Rupert Guinness, Doctors G. Stoker and Coleman, Miss MacDonnell, Nursing Sisters Walker, Denton,

Smyth, McGonigal, and Richardson, and Captain W.T. Mould, Royal Army Medical Corps.' Rupert was made a Companion of the Order of St Michael and St George (CMG) for distinguished contributions overseas, generally given then for colonial service. Annie McDonnell was decorated with the Royal Red Cross, awarded for exceptional services in military nursing; the first person to receive it had been Florence Nightingale.

Ned was pressed into the service of the Royal Family many more times, including on a visit of the Duke and Duchess of York to Dublin in 1899, when he brought them on a tour of the brewery in a motor car. He was always an early adopter of new technology, and cars were his new passion, which had amused the *Freeman's Journal*. He and one of his sons had been spotted

> going along Knightsbridge in a motor car, under the care of a driver wearing the customary anomalous yachting cap, which is the badge of the motor man. Lord Iveagh was evidently unused to the style of conveyance. His face had the expression of one who is waiting for something awkward to happen. He is evidently given to new ideas, for his shooting parties at Elvedon [*sic*] Hall this year have been connected by telephone with the House.

Queen Victoria died in January 1901 and the Prince of Wales succeeded her to the throne as Edward VII. Ned, as Lord Iveagh, swore allegiance to him in the House of Lords on 23 January, and to celebrate the coronation on 9 August 1902 (it had been delayed because of the new king's ill health) he threw a massive outdoor party for everyone who lived and worked on the estate at Elveden. Celebrations included a band and a cricket match, won easily by the village of Thetford with 73 runs in one innings, Elveden making only 59 in two. Ned and Adelaide, who were usually at Cowes for the sailing at that time of year, returned to London for the coronation itself, as did Arthur and Olive.

By August, Ned was back in Dublin for a meeting at the brewery. He had now resumed the chairmanship of the board, which he had given up along with his seat on the board in 1890, on the expiration of the three-year term agreed at the time of flotation. He had never fully stepped away, of course. His head would always have room for brewery matters, and he had remained up to date with developments and ever-ready to advise on decisions. In 1898 he had returned to the board, and within a few years the sudden illness and absence of the chairman, Adelaide's brother Reginald, created a vacancy which Ned was happy to fill.

It was still a flourishing business, and capacity was to double between 1901 and 1907. In Britain there was a huge appetite for Extra Stout, while porter was still popular in the home market. With turnover so good in Britain, and with Home Rule looking ever more likely, Ned and his fellow directors began to discuss the possibility of building a plant in England. This plan developed to the point where an option was bought on 100 acres at Trafford Park in Manchester, and the project was announced at the annual general meeting in 1913. It went down like a lead balloon in Dublin, but as things turned out, once war was declared in 1914, the plan was put on ice. Even after the war, the Manchester plant never did come to pass, but in the 1930s a brewery was built at Park Royal in west London, and it operated very successfully for 70 years.

When the king and queen visited Ireland in 1903, Ned suggested to them, more or less spontaneously, that they might like to visit the Iveagh Trust buildings. They agreed, and, in a move unknown in royal visits, prepared to visit those significantly deprived areas of the city, the Liberties and the Coombe. They completed an approving walkthrough of the new apartments of the Iveagh Trust, and were quite unexpectedly cheered heartily in the streets. The king even refused to get back into the carriage to be driven to St Patrick's, and insisted on walking, moving through the crowd of onlookers to do so. Nobody had expected

the visit to be such a success, and Ned was so pleased, and probably relieved, that he gave £50,000 to be divided between the
Dublin hospitals, regardless of religion. The following year the
royal couple returned to Dublin, and Ned and Adelaide gave
a giant dinner party for them at St Stephen's Green, for which
50 waiters were supposed to have been hired.

It might seem that there was little that could be added to the
Iveaghs' already overflowing cup, but 1903 also saw all three of
the 'boys' married: Walter to Lady Evelyn Erskine in early July,
Ernest to Miss Cloe Russell about two weeks later, and Rupert to
Lady Gwendolen Onslow, known as Gwennie, in October. Three
weddings in four months was a lot for any family to cope with,
no matter how much money there was to throw at the problem.
Gwennie, my great-grandmother, realised this some years later,
and wrote:

> among the very generous gift of household silver given
> to Rupert on his marriage by his parents, a number
> of silver candlesticks of Georgian design, but a recent
> hall-mark, I asked Mr. Bland [Lord Iveagh's private
> secretary], who told me that as we were third on the list,
> Lord Iveagh had already bought all the candlesticks he
> could find, and that he had had to be content with good
> copies for the third marriage!

In 1905, Ned received the news that he was to be raised a step in
the peerage and would become Viscount Iveagh, in recognition
of what he had done in, and for Ireland, and for the substantial
aid he had rendered through his public and philanthropic projects. But Ned's philanthropic work was nowhere near finished.
In Dublin, he engaged in a sequence of new building projects. By
1901 all the blocks in the Iveagh Trust's housing project in Kevin
Street were complete, and construction started in the Bull Alley
area beside St Patrick's. The new works were to include more

housing, in Patrick Street and Bride Street; the Iveagh House hostel already mentioned; the Iveagh Baths in Bride Street; and in 1911 construction began on the Guinness Trust Play Centre in Bull Alley.

The Play Centre was later named the Iveagh Play Centre, but always known locally as the Bayno, from 'beanfeast', meaning party. Ned had already set up another play centre at Myra Hall in Francis Street, near the Catholic church dedicated to St Nicholas of Myra. This new one, in Bull Alley, was built of fire-resistant reinforced concrete, although this was not obvious from the red-brick façade, dressed with pale limestone. It stood opposite St Patrick's, a beautiful situation which unfortunately necessitated the removal of some decorative plump cherubs who had been placed on some windowsills: nudity was not going to be tolerated that close to the cathedral.

The Play Centre was built to offer an after-school option for children from four to 14, the innovative idea being that children could continue to learn and to play in a safe and warm environment. A film taken there in 1954 shows children outside playing football and using a climbing frame and roundabout, and indoors whizzing down a slide, learning Irish dancing, playing chess and table tennis, as well as using the library and learning to sew and cook. A daily bun and a cup of cocoa were available to all the children who attended, and are remembered today in a traditional song about the Play Centre. There are several variations, but it is generally sung to the tune of 'Tiptoe Through the Tulips', with the lyric 'Tiptoe to the Bayno / Where the kids go / For their bun and cocoa / Tiptoe to the Bayno with me.' The Play Centre was a project in which Ned took a special personal interest, and he gifted £10,000 to it before it was vested in the trust.

Another project particularly close to Ned's heart, and one which he, rather than the trust, funded, was the pretty, red-bricked Iveagh Markets building. It was a little further away, fronting Francis Street and John Dillon Street, built of

Portmarnock brick with stone dressings. The steps and plinths were made of Newry granite, the door and window dressings and cornicing of Portland stone, and the keystones of the windows were carved with heads representing the nations of the world. It was designed and built to accommodate the hundreds of street traders who had stalls along Patrick Street and Francis Street and worked outdoors year-round, and contained both wet and dry market areas.

The dry market was accessible from Francis Street. At 100 feet wide by 150 feet long, its large central floor space was overlooked by a 15-foot-wide gallery running all the way around the inside of the building. The shops and stalls were divided by brick walls and fireproof partitions. Fire hydrants and hoses were distributed through the building, but any outbreak would be contained to a limited area. The entrance to the wet market, for fish, fruit and vegetables, was via John Dillon Street. The fish stalls were made of white glazed earthenware, and all the fittings designed to be easily cleaned. Each market had a refreshment room, kitchen, lavatories and hot and cold running water.

The designation of the new public markets had required an Act of Parliament, the Dublin Corporation Markets Act, 1901, which ruled out street trading on Ned's undertaking to provide suitable accommodation for the vendors within five years. He did so. The finished building was officially handed over to the Corporation in July 1906, when the keys to the market building were presented to the Lord Mayor. Trade was busy in the markets for 90 years, until they were closed by Dublin City Council (as Dublin Corporation had become) in 1996. The markets have lain derelict these 30 years. The original deed included a clause saying that the property would revert to the family if it were no longer being used as a market. I am actively pursuing the markets' return to social purpose, with the support of the people of the Liberties. Restoration of the decayed shell of the building is to be commenced by Dublin City Council in the autumn of 2025.

Meanwhile, at Elveden, the last significant building project the Iveaghs completed together was the enlargement and adornment of the medieval church at Elveden. Ned and Adelaide asked William Douglas Caröe, the most eminent ecclesiastical architect of his day, to design a new addition, with embellishments, to the village church. Caröe reroofed the whole church, and included a barrel ceiling over the chancel, adjacent to a double hammer-beam ceiling featuring carved angels, over the nave. Wooden east-of-England kings and saints adorn the pew ends, as well as various emblems, including snakes and shamrocks for St Patrick, and the thistle and saltire for St Andrew. The Iveaghs also commissioned from Frank Brangwyn a beautiful stained-glass window depicting Jesus's miracle in the provision of the loaves and fishes. The church of St Andrew & St Patrick was consecrated and dedicated on 8 October 1906. The doors of the church are open to all faiths today, and its other ornaments include those which celebrate Sikh lives, remembering the Maharaja and Maharani and their sons Frederick and Victor.

I imagine that it was at about this time that Ned and Adelaide – Ned and Dodo – chose to make Suffolk and Elveden their main base, a decision which would affect the lives and outlooks of so many of their descendants, myself included.

BRITISH ANTARCTIC EXPEDITION 1907.

9 REGENT STREET, WATERLOO PLACE.
LONDON, S.W.

TELEGRAPHIC ADDRESS
"ANTEXPEDI, LONDON"

TELEPHONE No.
9058 GERRARD.

The Lord Iveagh
5 Grosvenor Place. 17 . 7 . 07.

My Lord

I am most grateful
for your promise to guarantee
£2000 if other men will come
forward and guarantee the
rest of the £8000 we require
for the Expedition. Needless
to say that we will do all
in our power to make this,
the only British Expedition
going South, a complete success
for our Country

I am
my Lord —
Yours faithfully
Ernest H. Shackleton

Letter to Ned from Ernest Shackleton, 17 July 1907.

TWELVE

CHANGE OF SEASON

Ned's work in providing housing, improving working conditions and coming up with practical childcare solutions were crucial to the city-centre communities around St James's Gate and St Patrick's Cathedral south-east of the brewery. Even with the twentieth century well under way, Dublin was still bitterly impoverished, struggling with infant mortality, inadequate housing, poor sanitation and hunger. At the brewery, the range of supports offered to workers was now so broad that they were grouped together under 'Medical Department and Social Services'. Apart from services like dental and medical care, workers and their families were helped with every possible issue from financial services to advice and help given to children looking for work. The importance of exercise, usually in the context of the value of walking or riding to and from work, is a theme that recurs in the family letters, and became a theme in the brewery too. In 1905 Dr John Lumsden, the company's medical officer, founded the St James's Gate Athletic and Cycling Union, later called the Guinness Athletic Union, to which Ned would ultimately donate a site for a sports ground.

But while the brewery workers had access to these medical and social services, almost no other ordinary workers in the city did. Sir Charles Cameron, Dublin's medical inspector, reported in 1911 that, in the year to date, 206 children under the age of five had died in middle-class areas of Dublin, while 1,498 had died in poor areas. These were children to whom the Play Centre's daily cup of cocoa and bun, and safe place to play, might have made all the difference. That year, 26,000 people were living in overcrowded tenements in what were reputed to be the worst slums in Europe. The badly maintained and overcrowded housing stock which had convinced Ned to start the work of the Guinness Trust and the Iveagh Trust, hoping and believing that others in a position to do so would follow suit, had not vanished. In 1913, two terraced houses in Church Street collapsed, killing six people, including three young children. Dublin was not a city which could absorb much more strain, and yet it was constantly required to do so.

A huge labour dispute had been brewing in Dublin for some time, which centred around union membership. William Martin Murphy was a Home Ruler with multiple business interests, including several Catholic newspapers, Sackville Street's huge, luxurious department store Clery's, the Imperial Hotel and the Dublin United Tramways Company. The Dublin workforce was increasingly inspired by the passion and dedication of the social-ist union leaders Jim Larkin and James Connolly, who advocated for workers' improved pay and conditions and urged them to stand up for themselves and claim their rights, particularly the right to belong to a union.

Murphy, anxious about the growing influence of the Irish Transport and General Workers Union (ITGWU), which Larkin had co-founded, announced to those who worked for him that, unless they gave up their union membership, they would be refused access to their workplace. Four hundred other employ-ers followed suit in what became known as the Dublin Lockout. From August 1913 thousands of members of the urban workforce were prevented from accessing their workplaces and earning their living. The lockout lasted for six gruelling months. It was the biggest and bitterest industrial dispute in Ireland's history.

At the brewery no worker was locked out. It was the largest employer in the city, working conditions were excellent and it had already developed a good working relationship with the ITGWU. But its chairman, Ned, who so well understood that workers needed good housing, access to healthcare and childcare, and the benefits of leisure pursuits, also saw things from the employers' point of view. After a visit to the brewery by Murphy asking for money, Ned contributed £5,000 to the employers' fund. And while no one was sacked or locked out from Guinness for union membership, when Guinness boatmen refused to handle goods on the grounds that they came through strike-breakers, the crews were immediately sacked. Connolly personally asked Ernest Guinness to take them back, but neither Ernest nor Ned could see merit in that, wanting to make an example of the men.

The lockout ground on, until by January the workers were struggling. Demoralised by the refusal by the British Trades Union Congress to mount a sympathetic strike, the Dublin workforce began to return to work and sign the pledges put in front of them, unable to continue any longer without their incomes. Within the bigger story of the international labour movement, as well as within Dublin's story, the brewery's actions during the lockout do not indicate much sympathy with the workforce. Though on balance it was without a doubt one of the best employers to work for, if not the best, the brewery's situation was not perfect. Whatever errors of judgement were made during the lockout, they did not seem to mar the company's reputation in Dublin, and were perhaps outweighed by other, more impressive, behaviours by its management over many years.

John Redmond and the Irish Parliamentary Party had successfully campaigned for a new Home Rule Bill, which passed its first reading in 1912. The winds of change which had been blowing for many years now picked up, ready to sweep Ireland towards Home Rule and on to independence. In reaction, the year 1912 had seen the founding of the Ulster Volunteer Force, which soon grew to 100,000 men. Nearly 500,000 people signed the Ulster Covenant, swearing to use all means to defeat Home Rule. In response to that, the Irish Volunteers were formed. Their members ranged from Home Rulers to republicans, and came from a range of nationalist groups including the Gaelic League,

Sinn Féin, the Irish Republican Brotherhood, the Ancient Order of Hibernians and the Irish Parliamentary Party.

On New Year's Eve 1913, Rathmore wrote to Ned, referring to Ireland as 'a country where every man (on both sides) now carries a revolver (to say nothing of rifles &c.) – who can tell where the mischief would stop?' In Dublin, several Volunteers arranged for a consignment of rifles to be delivered from Germany, to be landed at Howth on the north side of Dublin Bay in July 1914. Marching back from Howth, Volunteers clashed with the Dublin Metropolitan Police and British soldiers, and the army fired on a group of jeering civilians on the Liffey quays. Four were killed and 37 were wounded. Membership of the Volunteers immediately rocketed.

That summer, war in Europe was edging closer too, but in Ned and Adelaide's corner of England the season progressed. King George V, who had succeeded to the throne in 1910, enjoyed his stays and his shoots at Elveden, like his late father. As Martelli put it:

> There was to be one more shooting season, not quite as good; one more London season; one more round of plea-sures and entertainments. And then, on 4th August 1914, the epoch which had produced Iveagh, and which in turn he had helped to form, came suddenly to its quiet and unprotesting end.

For the Iveaghs, as for so many families, the war's enormous loss of life in the trenches, the social flux and uncertainty, were hard to bear. Ned also had a deep personal consciousness that another era was coming to an end: in January 1915 his brother Arthur died, and in February 1916 Adelaide too. She had been unwell for some time, and so it did not come as a complete shock, but the loss was no less for that. The effect it had on Ned can be imagined; as Rupert's wife Gwendolen said of her parents-in-law: 'They were completely wrapped up in each other.' Ned himself had recognised this very early in their relationship. He told her in April 1873, before they were even married: 'You must never forget to write for you have made Ned so fond of Do that you have robbed him of all other interests', and, a couple of weeks later, 'I can take no interest in anyone no matter how I try'.

In stark contrast to the rich embellishment of the Iveaghs' church, Adelaide, the first Guinness to be buried in our family plot, has the simplest and smallest of gravestones. In time she would be joined by her widower, his grave similarly marked. Adelaide had died peacefully in her husband's arms, and her bedroom at Elveden remained untouched for the rest of Ned's life, including the flowers which had stood there at her passing. Ned commissioned a belfry and cloister of finest-quality flint workmanship, and the simple motto 'Sursum Corda' – our hearts are up – faces in the direction of the Hall. A full peal of bells would be delivered in 1921, and today these Elveden church bells are renowned, with bell-ringers coming from the entire length of England to enjoy them.

With one week's notice, Ned ceded a large part of Elveden to the War Ministry. The first tank crews were to be trained in this novel form of warfare in a top-secret area known as the Elveden High Explosives Area. They were inspected by the king and by the prime minister, prior to their breaking the deadlock in trench warfare, at the cost of almost all the tank crews' lives.

One thing Ned did not have to worry about was money, and although these reported chart-toppings are usually wild guesses, the *Daily Express* described him in 1914 as the richest man in England. Most people, the newspaper said, would think of the Rothschilds as the richest, but 'although the collective wealth of the Rothschild family is almost beyond all computation, no individual member is nearly as rich as Lord Iveagh.'

The brewery continued to improve its profits, from £1,280,505 at the start of the war to over £2,000,000 in 1918. By 1921 they were at their highest-ever of £3,729,803. So he was in a position to spend freely in areas he felt it was warranted. He directed much of his war spending to hospitals, including building and maintaining a new wing at the Netley (Royal Victoria) Hospital near Southampton, and new accommodation at St Bricin's (George V) Hospital in Arbour Hill in Dublin. He also told the Irish Red Cross that, if they needed to equip any spare wards in the Royal City of Dublin Hospital in Baggot Street, he would pay for them, and this brought 167 beds into use.

Ernest was now at the brewery in Dublin, where he had been vice-chairman since 1913, but the war would take Rupert to Canada with the Naval Reserves, and Walter to France, where Schomberg McDonnell, Salisbury's brilliant secretary and Rupert's best man, died in the trenches in November 1915. The following September, Ned gave a snapshot of the war's horror in a letter to Rupert:

> Walter was with his regiment ... for 6 weeks in the fire trench near Thiepval – at the end of that time they were quite worn out and had lost 90 men killed and wounded and have now been sent back to rest and fill up the ranks with new men – So he is now safe for at least about a fortnight.

During the war, Ned lost not only his wife but a swathe of brewery employees, with fathers, brothers and sons slaughtered. In the style of Nelson's Column in Trafalgar Square, Ned commissioned the Elveden War Memorial which stands where the parish boundaries of Elveden, Eriswell and Icklingham meet. Nearly 130 feet tall, this memorial carries the names of all those locals who lost their lives in the Great War. Many surnames are repeated, illustrating just how common it was for families to lose several men. These men's names are ordered by parish, facing their respective communities. Field Marshal Sir Henry Wilson unveiled this memorial in 1921. The following year, he was assassinated outside his London home by two members of the Irish Republican Army.

Curtains were falling everywhere. For Ireland's union with Great Britain, it looked like just a matter of time. Home Rule at last came into law in 1914, but its implementation was suspended by the outbreak of war. When the armed rebellion erupted in Dublin, on Easter Monday 1916, two months after Adelaide's death, Ned was still in the haze of his grief. He described the Rising, which lasted for six days, as having happened 'because they knew there were only 4,000 soldiers in the Country and they had very few guns and hardly any ammunition'. Fifteen revolutionary leaders were executed within a nine-day period, and Sir Roger Casement was hanged at Pentonville a few months later. Although there were many in Ireland who had not even been sure what was going on during the Rising, and plenty of republicans who did not support it, the executions sent grief, shock and outrage coursing through the country. Ned may not have wanted to believe in the possibility of a republican future, but the aftermath of the Rising swung the general public sentiment in Ireland.

In December 1917 Lord Rathmore told Ned in a letter that he had bumped into Edward Carson, Asquith's attorney-general and a passionate Unionist, at the Carlton Club and heard from him that 'the rank and file of the loyalists there [in Ulster] had been hardened and made more uncompromising by the toleration of the Sinn Feiners by the Government'. The idea that the government had taken a softly-softly approach to the republican cause was not generally held. John Dillon MP, a member of the Irish Parliamentary Party, told the House of Commons: 'In the whole of modern history ... there has been no rebellion or insurrection put down with so much blood and so much savagery as the recent insurrection in Ireland.'

Hard lines were drawn. Irish nationalists did not intend to accept a Home Rule that excepted Ulster, and Ulster Unionists did not intend to be a minority in a new Irish parliament. It was Unionism of a kind which the anxiously conciliatory Ned, now in his 70s, had never embraced nor foreseen. In the general election of 1918 Sinn Féin swept the board. Countess Markiewicz, who had spent a long time imprisoned in Holloway and Aylesbury after the Rising, became the first woman to be elected an MP, though as Sinn Féin was abstentionist she refused to take the oath of allegiance to the Crown and did not take her seat in the House of Commons. (Lady Astor, the daughter-in-law of Waldorf Astor, who had been a guest at shooting parties at Elveden, won a by-election in 1919 and became the first woman to take a seat.)

There was more pain and struggle ahead for Ireland, in the form of the War of Independence from 1919 to 1921, the partition of the country under the Anglo-Irish Treaty of 1921, and the birth of the Irish Free State in 1922. The new state decided to adopt as its symbol the Brian Boru harp, named for the Irish king who defeated the Vikings at the Battle of Clontarf in the eleventh century. There was a difficulty, though, which was that under Benjamin Lee's guidance, the brewery had in the 1860s begun to use the Brian Boru harp design on its labelling. More than that, it had trademarked the harp symbol. The new state had to flip the design and use a left-facing harp instead.

One strand of Ned's life which an increase in his time and resources enabled him to explore through the last 20 years or so of his life was his endless thirst for knowledge and discovery, and his passionate support for research and education. In 1896 a dog bit one of the Elveden grooms, Jim Jackson. This led to Ned's sending Jackson to a French medical facility, at that time the only one in the world able to offer treatment for rabies. There, he made a full recovery following treatment, and the episode was the catalyst for Ned's making an outsize donation of £250,000 to the British Institute for Preventive Medicine. This enabled the Lister Institute, as it was renamed in 1903, to take a leading role in the decades-long fight against infectious diseases as causes of death, and it grew to become one of the world's most important biomedical research institutes.

Numerous discoveries were made by Lister staff, and their success was recognised with awards and prizes; the institute's first head of chemistry, Arthur Harden, won a Nobel Prize in 1929. Lister investigators defined and coined the term 'vitamin', described the ABO blood groups that now allow safe blood transfusions, and identified the cause of rickets. The Lister played a central role in the eradication of smallpox, the treatment of tetanus and gas gangrene. Achievements in more recent years include the successful patent applications arising from Crick and Watson's discovery of DNA. Further income flowed to the institute following Sir Alec Jeffreys's extraordinary breakthrough in DNA technology, when he developed the genetic profiling that would be widely used as a forensic tool.

Since Ned's first intervention in 1896, members of my family have continuously contributed to the Lister through membership of its board. Today, the institute is well established as a research funder, and it grants in the region of £300,000 annually to successful applicants to carry out, with considerable freedom, scientific research across a range of areas, from basic biology to clinical fields, including infection, neuroscience, cancer and genetic disorders. Since 1982, more than 150 Lister Research Fellows have made an impact on human health, often focusing on areas still in their infancy. A recent Trinity College Dublin fellowship, for example, resulted in research on memory engrams, to better understand whether – and how – misplaced infant memories are retrieved in adults.

In 1907 Ned took the opportunity of funding scientific research of a different kind: the British Antarctic Expedition. He received in July a letter from the Duke of Westminster which introduced Lieutenant Shackleton:

> who did such fine service in the last expedition to the South Pole. He is taking an expedition there himself: his ship and crew are ready, but he is unable to start unless £8,000 can be guaranteed to him. He is quite of the opinion that the guarantee will never be called on for repayment.

The Shackletons were originally from Yorkshire, but Ernest's father had settled to farm in Kilkea in county Kildare, about

25 miles from Oughterard. The family had moved to London when Ernest was still a child, but his biographer Roland Huntford described him as a lifelong 'Irishman in England', also mentioning how persuasive he was, with 'a capacity to hide shrewd calculation under onion skins of charm'. Ned was shrewd enough to insist on something more than charm, and Shackleton provided him with testimonials as to his ability and character, along with an already remarkable curriculum vitae. This included details of his 1901–03 Antarctic voyage on the *Discovery* with Captain Robert Scott, when he had accompanied Scott on the sledge journey which had beaten the Farthest South record. He and Ned had several things in common: they shared a connection with Kildare, and they were both hugely capable, driven Irish men in England, both riveted by the possibilities for expanding human knowledge.

Westminster himself was prepared to guarantee £2,000 for the expedition, and Ned agreed to match it. The final £4,000 would be guaranteed by Sir Rupert Clarke and Lady Brocklehurst. Shackleton arranged the details of signing the bank guarantee with Ned's secretary. This was signed in July 1907 and the document itself survives. Shackleton wrote his thanks to Ned directly, and some months later, in January 1908, he wrote to him again, this time from the *Nimrod*. He used as an address his co-ordinates of 78° 30 S, 172° W, in McMurdo Sound:

> I just write to you a line to tell you that so far the Expedition is getting all right, we are now off the great Ice Barrier and hope soon to reach our winter quarters.
>
> I have had a heavy time as nearly every day since the vessel left N Zealand we have had heavy gales; indeed I have not yet taken my clothes off. I hope soon to have a rest when we have our hut landed and the stores ashore.

Shackleton was keen to reassure Ned that his confidence was merited and that the expedition was going to be a success. 'It is a long walk to the South Pole but I hope to do it. You will hear of the Expedition in March 1909 all being well.' The expedition did not in the end reach the South Pole, but did set a new Farthest South record. Shackleton was rewarded for his efforts with a knighthood.

In November 1909 Shackleton sent Ned a copy of his book, and referred him to the map pages. 'You will see your mountain on the map it is over 9000 feet but I did not put the height as we are uncertain.' It was the newly named Antarctic mountain, Mount Iveagh. Ned wrote to thank Shackleton, and to congratulate him on his knighthood, but he did not provide any further finance, and when Shackleton contacted him with details of a mining investment, he was not interested.

Other scientific research work was closer to home for Ned, both literally and figuratively. Finding the estate suddenly, if temporarily, in the use of the War Office, and wondering what the future held may have forced him to think about the challenge of how to make the land productive. It is generally regarded as a mark of the potential seen in my family's occupation of Elveden that our estate was, largely, returned to us. Much local land was to be taken under the control of the newly formed Forestry Commission, and dedicated to the production of timber – a key national resource in short supply.

This narrow escape from state nationalisation highlighted to Ned, and to Rupert, who was already interested in innovations in agriculture, the need to think afresh about the land, or risk losing it. Ned realised that there was a significant lack of structured, practical training for those who wanted to work on the land. Ned bought the beautiful 522-acre Chadacre Estate, near Shimpling in Suffolk, about 15 miles from Elveden.

Here, in 1920, he endowed the Chadacre Agricultural Institute, which opened its doors at the end of September 1921. It offered a diverse range of agriculture and food-based courses to farm labourers, small-holders and small farmers. Applicants had to be resident in Suffolk, and the costs of the instruction and training courses, as well as board and lodging, were covered. In an understanding that for farm workers, absence from the land had to fall within the seasonal patterns of their work, training took place over two winter periods of six months each.

The Great War had demonstrated a significant shortage of domestically produced food and materials: only one third of the food consumed in the United Kingdom was produced there. Chadacre was one of the first agricultural training colleges in the country, and after Adelaide's death in 1916, four years before its purchase, Ned spent much of his last ten years planning and executing the operation of the institute. A committee of educationalists and notable local land practitioners was assembled to devise the curriculum.

The Chadacre students divided their time between science laboratory, lecture theatre and the institute's farm, but their timetable included a range of social and sporting activities in addition to the focus on agricultural learning. The ethos of the institute was holistic. Similarly to the brewery in Dublin, it did not simply provide a work place, but remained cognisant of the complexity of individual lives, and of the long-term benefits and importance of nurturing a person's many aspects.

Rupert Guinness never lost his interest in the land. He pioneered the use of innovative agricultural techniques at his own new home, Pyrford Court, which he and Gwendolen built in 1903. At the nearby Hoebridge Farm in Woking, he also founded an Emigration Training School for farm workers, to prepare them for farm life elsewhere, with particular emphasis on Canada, Australia and New Zealand. The farm was equipped with Canadian implements and equipment, and livestock, like pedigree cows and Tamworth pigs, which were popular in Canada. Later, Gwendolen oversaw a women's training school with practical classes in bottling fruit, making jam, and doing poultry and dairy work.

The Chadacre Agricultural Institute ran until 1990, when the trustees, chaired by my late father, elected to close it. After a successful sale of its assets, they constituted the Chadacre Agricultural Trust, which benefits a whole range of land-based activities, including school visits to farms and rural showcase days, agricultural and scientific training and land-related innovation. In 2024, a typical year, the Chadacre Trust awarded nearly £200,000 to deserving persons and projects within the four East of England counties of Suffolk, Norfolk, Essex and Cambridgeshire. Chadacre students have gone on to hold key positions within land-based industries, and its role in progressing a diverse range of disciplines which constitute the spectrum of modern agriculture cannot be emphasised enough. It has been my personal privilege to chair this charity, following on from my late Papa, Benjamin, who vacated the role in 1992.

Ned did not neglect education in Dublin, and donated about £50,000 for various facilities at Trinity College Dublin, including the Physics Building, the Botany Building and Trinity Hall, a hall of residence which was at that time for women only. In 1908 he was offered, and accepted, the Chancellorship of Trinity College Dublin. That same year saw the establishment of the National University of Ireland to cater for Catholics, whose archbishop at the time had forbidden them to attend Trinity without first seeking special dispensation. Augustine Birrell, the Chief Secretary for Ireland, wanted Ned's back garden in St Stephen's Green, and perhaps even his house, for the new university. He wrote to Ned's friend Walter Long to propose the idea. Long immediately forwarded the letter to Ned, who returned it with the tart reply:

> It is quite frank and to me personally quite friendly and in the same frank and friendly spirit I had better at once say that his suggestion is one that I could not for a moment entertain.

He did later have a change of heart, perhaps aware of the potential impact of the gesture of the provision of a site for a Catholic

University by the Church of Ireland Chancellor of Trinity. It was not enough of a change of heart to make him hand over his beloved home, nor even one of the stretch of four houses through which that home now extended, but it was enough for him to grant a site behind his stables. The Dublin college of the National University was built there, accessed via Earlsfort Terrace to the east.

The 1920s saw Ned, understandably, living a much quieter and more secluded life than he had before the war and before Adelaide's death; he never resumed the full scale or pattern of the life that had given them so much pleasure over the years. In a gesture of the love and understanding that had outlasted any passing brotherly frustrations, Arthur, with Olive's agreement, had left Ashford to Ned, because he thought the estate would be too much of a burden on Olive, and that Ned 'was the person best fitted to deal with them'. So Ned returned to Ashford and the estate that Benjamin Lee had so enjoyed, and he spent time there shooting woodcock. He still liked to have a few people down to shoot at Elveden too, and the king resumed his visits in 1919, the same year he conferred Ned with an earldom. Ned accepted the honour, while writing to the king: 'I have done nothing to earn or deserve such a reward.'

The new Earl of Iveagh continued to take pleasure in the sport himself, though his physical health sometimes intervened. 'I find I am slow with my gun,' he wrote to Rupert in 1923, hoping that Rupert would be able to take his place in the line when the king came to shoot the following week. He did not spend as much time in Dublin now, though he did go to Farmleigh every year in late summer, and he still travelled, making trips to Paris and to the United States, where he had some property investments.

Before his death, he had one more project to organise, and that was the Georgian beauty Kenwood House, on the edge of Hampstead Heath. The house and grounds were about to be sold for development, and in 1925 Ned bought them, with the intention of leaving them to London County Council to make a permanent art gallery. In preparation for this he moved many of his own paintings into Kenwood, listing 40 which were to stay with the house.

In a strange echo of Sir Hugh Lane's bequest of his paintings, Ned neglected to have the relevant codicil to his will witnessed. Sorting this out eventually required an Act of Parliament, and it was this that prompted Bryan Guinness to argue for a similar solution for the Hugh Lane paintings. Today, Kenwood House, still operating, as Ned had insisted it should, without any admission charge, is one of London's leading visitor attractions. Its astonishing collection includes masterpieces by Vermeer and Rembrandt.

In an extraordinary bridge between the old order and the new, when Ned was at Farmleigh in August 1927, he had Mr and Mrs William Cosgrave to tea. Cosgrave had been a Sinn Féin member, had founded Cumann na nGaedheal (the precursor to today's Fine Gael party) and was now President of the Executive Council – that is, the Irish Free State's head of government. He had been imprisoned after the Rising, and sentenced to death, though this had been commuted.

The political situation in Ireland was still far from steady, and only the previous month Cosgrave's vice-president and long-time collaborator, Kevin O'Higgins, had been murdered by members of the Irish Republican Army. By way of security, guards hid in the shrubbery on either side of Farmleigh's drive, and a cavalcade of motorbikes escorted Mr and Mrs Cosgrave to the front door. Ned joked with Cosgrave about the last time he had seen him, when he had also had an armed guard, but that time he had been under arrest by the British police.

It was a colourful moment in what was to be Ned's last trip to Ireland. On his return to London he developed phlebitis in his right leg, and about ten days later he died, aged 79. He is buried beside Adelaide, at Elveden.

* * *

The Guinness story does not, of course, end there, but just as I had to choose the point at which to make an incision in time to start the story with Arthur Guinness in Oughterard, so I have to find an end point. For Elveden, things began to open up in a completely different way after Ned's death. Under Rupert's hand, those unproductive fields were transformed, and for a hundred years now the estate has been largely farmland.

Most of the family property in Ireland mentioned in this book is now in state ownership, some accessible to the public and some not. At St Anne's, the house no longer exists. But the grounds are a public park and you can still see the old follies, including the bridge built by Benjamin Lee, so full of joy when his daughter Annie Lee was born. Ashford has been converted into a five-star hotel, with a dining room named in memory of that 1905 shooting party when Arthur hosted the Prince of Wales, bagging his woodcock, snipe and duck in Ballykine Wood and Lough Mask.

Farmleigh, where Ned and Adelaide went as newlyweds, and where I was born, is in the hands of the Office of Public Works. It functions as the official Irish State Guesthouse. The St Stephen's Green mansion originally bought by Benjamin Lee, and so dramatically and expensively extended by Ned, is the headquarters of the Department of Foreign Affairs and now called Iveagh House. Behind it, the pretty Iveagh Gardens are open to the public, and dogs delightedly chase tennis balls across the sunken archery ground laid out for the exhibition of 1865.

It is impossible to imagine what Dublin would be like without Arthur's great gift, St Stephen's Green, operating day and night, as he wanted it to, as the city's lung; impossible to imagine Dublin 8 without the characteristic red brick of the Iveagh Play Centre (now the Liberties College), the Iveagh Buildings, Baths and Markets; impossible to imagine not hearing from St Patrick's Park the bells of St Patrick's Cathedral. And it is impossible for me, and perhaps for any Dubliner, to imagine it without the great brewery, still an industrial campus in the city centre, still employing Dubliners, still sending Guinness anywhere people will drink it and every year contributing hundreds of millions of euros to the Irish exchequer.

I have run down the spine of the family for this book, and that has meant that whole branches of the family are not included. It has also resulted in a story that is largely male, although so many fascinating and capable women have also been involved. The book had to have a shape and a central narrative, and if I had included all the people and all the stories it would never have made it to print.

As well as people, this is very much a book about place, which is why I made that trip to Oughterard at the outset, and why Dublin herself is a central character in the story. Our family story, like so many Irish family stories, has played out amid an extraordinary sequence of historical events. Arthur Guinness left Kildare before the canals and railways transformed its connection with Dublin and the rest of the country, lived through the 1798 Rebellion, and the Act of Union which merged the Irish and British parliaments. He did not live to see Catholic Emancipation, as his children did.

His great-grandson Ned, born in 1847, the worst year of the Famine, shot countless (or rather, carefully counted) partridge with the British king and took tea with the first head of government of the Irish Free State. There seems to have been no point in this whole story at which Ireland was a country at peace, and yet these many generations of my family found peace in it, as I do myself. I am always touched to see the many ways in which my family's story is remembered at home, always delighted that it means as much to other people as it does to me.

Brendan Moore with Elveden Ale, 2025.

EPILOGUE

'Whoever could make two ears of corn or two blades of grass to grow upon a spot of ground where only one grew before would deserve better of mankind and do more essential service to his country than the whole race of politicians put together.'

– Jonathan Swift, *Gulliver's Travels*

This is one of my favourite quotations, and for as long as I can remember my father kept these lines, written out in careful calligraphy, at home at Elveden. Jonathan Swift, who was Dean of St Patrick's Cathedral, which my ancestor Benjamin Lee Guinness restored in the 1860s, was perhaps a little harsh on politicians (more or less required in a satirist), but I've always thought he was on to something about crop yields – particularly, from the perspective of my own family, barley.

No one was growing maize in Ireland in 1726, when *Gulliver's Travels* was published, and when Swift speaks here of 'corn' he means cereal crops generally. Gulliver uses 'corn' and 'barley' interchangeably when talking about his experience in the land of the giants, Brobdingnag, and at one point he walks through a field of barley rising 40 feet high.

At Elveden, we haven't quite managed that yet, but we're not doing too badly with our crop. Our brewer, Brendan Moore, malts the barley from the farm – this malting process encourages the harvested grain to germinate, the first step towards great beer. Brendan brews both Elveden ale and stout, and we sell them from our two village pubs, the Guinness Arms (the only Guinness

Arms in the world) and the Elveden Inn. You can also get a pint of Guinness there, naturally, and it's about the same alcohol strength as the Elveden beers.

Brendan produces 1.4 pints of beer per square foot of barley we grow, or nearly 15 and a half pints of beer per square metre of harvested barley grains. Each acre of barley we grow here yields an average of 25,340 pints of beer, or, if you prefer, each hectare yields 62,600 pints.

Not all our Elveden barley becomes Elveden beer, because we also have a long-term association with Diageo, now makers of Guinness, and we supply them with barley too. So, although we no longer run the brewery at St James's Gate, we are still turning barley into beer. It seems to be in the blood.

ACKNOWLEDGEMENTS

This book would have been far more difficult without the assiduous record-keeping of my late father Benjamin Guinness and the custodianship of my great-grandfather Rupert Guinness. The work of author George Martelli, who was commissioned by Rupert to record the family history, was invaluable in writing it.

It would have been impossible without the vigour and profound research of Dr Antonia Hart.

My thanks go to David Dickson, Emeritus Professor of Modern History, Trinity College Dublin; Dr Jason McElligott, Keeper, Marsh's Library Dublin; and to Stephen Naughton.

My thanks extend to my siblings, Emma, Louisa and Rory, whose encouragement in so many various ways means so much to me.

This book would not have come about as it has without Henry Channon, my late childhood friend and cousin, business partner, and lover of the arts, which led him to own Scala Publishers for a number of years.

It would not have been conceived at all without the care, love and professional acumen of Katie Channon.

Profound personal thanks to publisher Polly Powell, James Kellow, Mia Autumn Roe and Jane Pickett, and the care of my editor Oliver Craske, and all the wonderful team at Batsford/Scala who get the point of this all. I am indebted to the great patience and forbearance of Gill Hastings in my office at Elveden; and to Eibhlin Colgan and Leanne Harrington of the Guinness Storehouse, who have been immensely helpful. And here's to the patient research and authorship of cousin Patrick and Joe Joyce, and so many others. Indeed, many other persons have contributed in so many ways, too many to mention here.

FURTHER READING

Books about the Guinness family

Bryan Guinness, *Dairy Not Kept: Essays in Recollection* (Compton Press, 1975).

Patrick Guinness, *Arthur's Round: the Life and Times of Brewing Legend Arthur Guinness* (Peter Owen, 2014).

Joe Joyce, *The Guinnesses: the Untold Story of Ireland's Most Successful Family* (Poolbeg, 2009).

Patrick Lynch and John Vaizey, *Guinness's Brewery in the Irish Economy, 1759–1876* (Cambridge University Press, 1960).

George Martelli, *Man of his Time* (privately printed, 1957).

Frederic Mullally, *The Silver Salver* (Granada, 1981).

Derek Wilson, *Dark and Light: the Story of the Guinness Family* (Weidenfeld & Nicolson, 1998).

Other books

Bernadette Cunningham, *Medieval Irish Pilgrims to Santiago de Compostela* (Four Courts Press, 2018).

Angelique Day, ed., *Letters from Georgian Ireland: the correspondence of Mary Delany, 1731–68* (Friar's Bush Press, 1991).

David Dickson, *Dublin: The Making of a Capital City* (Profile, 2014).

Frances Gerard, *Picturesque Dublin: Old and New* (Hutchinson, 1898).

J.T. Gilbert, *A History of the City of Dublin*, vol. III (McGlashan and Gill, 1859).

Samuel Carter Hall and Anna Maria Hall, *Ireland, its Scenery, Character and History* (Hall, Virtue 1850).

John Hely-Hutchinson, *Commercial Restraints of Ireland*, Ninth Letter, Dublin, 10th Sept., 1779.

Frederick Douglas How, *William Conyngham Plunket: fourth Baron Plunket and sixty-first Archbishop of Dublin, A Memoir* (Isbister, 1900).

Elizabeth Malcolm, *'Ireland Sober, Ireland Free': Drink and Temperance in 19th Century Ireland* (Syracuse University Press and Gill & Macmillan, 1986).

Violet Martin, *Irish Memories: the Martins of Ross* (1917).

John James McGregor, *New picture of Dublin: comprehending a history of the city, an accurate account of its various establishments and institutions, and a correct description of all the public edifices connected with them; with an appendix containing several useful tables; forming a complete guide to everything curious and interesting in the Irish metropolis* (Dublin, 1821).

Asenath Nicholson, *Annals of the famine in Ireland, in 1847, 1848, and 1849* (French, 1851).

Barnaby Rich, *A new Description of Ireland, together with the Manners, Customs, and Dispositions of the People* (London, 1610).

Jeffery Vail, *The Literary Relationship of Lord Byron and Thomas Moore* (Johns Hopkins, 2001).

Chapters and articles

H.F. Berry, 'Notes from the Diary of a Dublin Lady in the Reign of George II', *The Journal of the Royal Society of Antiquaries of Ireland*, Fifth Series, Vol. 8, No. 2 (30 June 1898), 141–54.

Lena Boylan, 'Celbridge in Vanessa's Time', *Journal of the County Kildare Archaeological Society*, Vol. XVI No. 5, 1985/6.

Leanne Calvert, 'The Journal of John Tennent, 1786–90', *Analecta Hibernica*, No. 43 (2012), 69–128.

Oliver Macdonagh 'The Origins of Porter', *The Economic History Review*, 16(3) (1964), 530–35.

Elizabeth Malcolm, 'The Catholic Church and the Irish Temperance Movement, 1838–1901', *Irish Historical Studies* 23, no. 89 (1982): 1–16.

Desmond F. Moore, 'The Guinness Saga', *Dublin Historical Record* 16, no. 2 (1960): 50–57.

Mary O'Dowd, 'History of Children and Childhood, 1700–1800', Museum of Childhood https://museumofchildhood.ie/history-of-children-and-childhood-1700-1800/

Rosemary Raughter, '"A Time of Trial Being near at Hand": Pregnancy, Childbirth and Parenting in the Spiritual Journal of Elizabeth Bennis, 1749–79', in *'She Said She Was in the Family Way': Pregnancy and Infancy in Modern Ireland*, edited by Elaine Farrell, 75–90. (University of London Press, 2012).

INDEX

Illustrations are in *italics*. Plate numbers ('*P*') refer to the page of the plate section on which that image appears. All places are in Dublin unless stated otherwise.